WHAT OTHERS ARE SAYING ABOUT
Wounded to Wonderful

Wounded to Wonderful is a deep dive into the emotions of the soul. Pastor John Braland lays bare his personal journey with emotional pain, depression, hurt, anger and shame in order to shine the light of healing Scriptures upon them as he has experienced in his own journey from wounded to wonderful.

Writing with openness and brutal honesty, John invites the reader to "do something about their own pain, suffering and shame" and to experience the healing truths of Holy Scripture through the presence and power of the Holy Spirit.

Pastor John shares his sufferings and the source of healing in his own life in order that others in the Body of Christ, the Church, may experience healing, too, in their journey from wounded to wonderful. It is a must read.

PASTOR FRANK MASSERANO
Founding Pastor
International Ministerial Fellowship

In this world we all encounter trouble, some of which wounds us so deeply that we become wrecks. Pastor John Braland navigates his own journey of discovering wounds that negatively impacted his life and shares how he went from wounded to wonderful and how you can too. This is an inspiring read for all who are wounded and want to find wonderful in their lives.

GLENN HAGGERTY,
Author

Everyone who comes to Jesus Christ in relationship and desires to grow will need to face their own past in honesty. In John's new book, *Wounded to Wonderful*, he helps us face our past with the level of integrity needed to set us free from all that hinders, and forges a new path ahead of us for a future filled with abundance.

As a skillful surgeon who first searches the wound and relates the real condition, he leads us gently into our past fear, anger, shame & regrets, offering strong Biblical examples and practical Scriptures to help set us free. Then, as an authentic guide who has gone ahead on the path, beckons us with personal applications to help re-center us on our true identity as sons and daughters of the Almighty.

My favorite line in the book is, "Allow the Holy Spirit to work in your woundedness and allow Him to move you to a place of wonderfulness." I highly recommend this book to all.

REV. CARL WESLEY ANDERSON,
Equipping Evangelist and Media Missionary, Author of, *Love Speaks* and Executive Producer of twin TV Series, *Love Speaks* on TBN, and *From History to Hope* on *GOD-TV* and other Christian Networks world-wide.

Encouraging and insightful! There is much to be learned from Dr. Braland as he shares his heart through personal stories and experiences. *Wounded to Wonderful* gives practical exercises and is engaging from the introduction to the very last page as it leads the reader through the necessary steps to heal from life hurts. This book will be a great resource for our ministry to use as we work with teens and families in personal healing and reconciling relationships.

CINDY MCKITTRICK,
Executive Director, Hope Harbor

As a senior health care executive this book speaks to all of us as leaders, healers, and individuals not just in the service of our organizations, teams and patients but to our individual journey to be our most joyful and healthiest selves. It guides us to ask introspective questions and find answers from our heart and soul. This book provides teachings and tools for you to identify your personal wounds, acknowledge them, then accept and grow. As a daughter, sister, wife, mother and grandmother, the book applies to all stages of life. As a reader, you start your journey with the authentic sharing of the author's story. It invites us to journey with him reflecting on our own story, as we heal our own wounds, creating our most wonderful selves; the life Jesus uniquely designed us to live.

THERESA PESCH, RN

WOUNDED
to
WONDERFUL

International Standard Book Number
978-1-7341023-0-7 (print)
978-1-7341023-1-4 (ebook)

Braland Ministries
4319 Steiner Street
St. Bonifacius, Minnesota, 55375

Cover and Interior Designs: Nan Bishop nbishopsdesigns@cox.net

Printed in the United States of America
Original Printing October 2019

DEDICATION

This book is dedicated to my wife, Kathi, who loves me and supports me. It is also dedicated to my kids—Josh, Sara, and Katie—who I love and cherish more than words can express.

CONTENTS

FOREWORD

This book has been written for those who have experienced emotional wounds, hurts, disappointments, anger, frustration, and unforgiveness toward self and others, and have suffered.

It's a deep dive into a psychological and spiritual study of emotional responses to what some might call human mood disorders, including depression, anger and shame. And the author assumes the reader wants to change and move from woundedness to wonderful.

I suppose what is described here is largely the human condition as experienced by most all of us. It's part of living. All of us have experienced some of it at one time or another, some of us much more than we care to admit. The author asks the question, "What do you, the reader, want to do about it?"

We need redemptive healing, and God is the only source from which we can experience that healing of soul, body, and mind.

Sometimes we need help with spiritual and cognitive direction. Pastor John Braland provides that help with insightful, practical, and biblical truth.

The gift of teaching is evident as Pastor Braland guides us through a morass of negative human emotions. Along the way, he offers positive Scriptural anecdotes that open our understanding to biblical truth and the healing presence of the Holy Spirit. God loves, God heals, He has a purpose for your life, and it's for good

(Jeremiah 29:11, Romans 8:28). He has provided a remedy and a path to wholeness for us as we:

- ◉ Identify our wounds
- ◉ Experience trust over deceit
- ◉ Release our fears
- ◉ Learn to turn away from anger
- ◉ Forsake shame and embrace redemption
- ◉ Release loss and embrace life
- ◉ Discover healthy rhythms
- ◉ Learn to practice soul care
- ◉ Experience continuing health

This book is uniquely John's experiences and life. He has sacrificed his personal privacy in order to share the lessons he has learned with the reader. I have heard John say, "There are new experiences in which we can discover God's healing grace; if we're not dead, God's not finished with us yet." Through the work of the Holy Spirit in you, you too can become a living testimony and witness of your journey from wounded to wonderful. (Col. 1:24-27)

PASTOR FRANK MASSERANO, M.DIV., TH.M.
Founding Pastor
International Ministerial Fellowship

Acknowledgments

Many people have encouraged, led, supported, and helped me be the person that I am.

Kathi Braland is my soul mate and best friend.

Dan Sorensen is a godly friend who knows all my warts.

Leith Anderson is an outstanding role model for me.

Larry Osborne speaks the truth and has always given me new insight.

Frank Messarano taught me humility and how to love others.

Vanessa Martinson encouraged me to be real all the time.

Glenn Haggerty has been a friend, mentor, and confidant for years. He is also a gifted writer who helped bring this book to fruition.

My church staff is awesome and loves to do ministry together.

Carrie Carlson always kept it clean and simple in the editing process.

My dog Hunter has always made time to listen.

Freshwater Church (where I serve) is full of incredible people. They are inspiring and challenging. It is an honor to serve with them.

Special thank you to John Williams at Lakeside Pottery for providing the pottery on the cover. To purchase your own Kintsugi pottery, visit lakesidepottery.com.

INTRODUCTION

A man was looking for a job and noticed there was an opening at the local zoo. He inquired about the job and discovered that the zoo had a very unusual position to fill. Apparently their gorilla had died and, until they could get a new one, they needed someone to dress up in a gorilla suit and act like a gorilla for a few days. His job would be to sit, eat, and sleep. His identity would be kept a secret. Thanks to a very fine gorilla suit, no one would be the wiser. The zoo offered good pay for this job, so the man decided to do it. He tried on the suit and sure enough, he looked just like a gorilla. They led him to the cage where he took a position at the back of the cage and pretended to sleep. But after a while he got tired of sitting, so he walked around a little bit, jumped up and down, and tried a few gorilla noises. The people watching seemed to really like that. When he would move or jump around, they would clap and cheer. So, he jumped around a little more and even tried climbing a tree. Now the crowd was really into him. Playing to the crowd, he grabbed a vine and swung from one side of the cage to the other. The people loved it, so he swung higher and higher and the crowd grew bigger and bigger. Then all of a sudden the vine broke, launching him up and out of the cage, and causing him to crash squarely into the middle of the lion's cage. This woke the lion, and the man in the gorilla suit panicked. He started jumping up and down, screaming and yelling, "Help, help! Get me out of here! I'm a man in a gorilla suit! Help!" The lion eyed him and slowly walked toward him. When the lion was four feet away it pounced on the man in the gorilla suit. The lion opened its strong jaws as if to take a big bite of a tasty gorilla. Then a voice came out of the lion's mouth "Will you shut up! You're gonna to get us both fired!"

As a society we have gotten really good at being really fake. We have conditioned ourselves to cover our wounds with a veneer of false pride and a dollop of disconnect. We learn to mask pain, failures, depression, anxiety, fear, problems, burnout, and even spiritual emptiness. I have gone off to more than one obligatory social event completely broken inside while boldly telling others that I was entirely blessed. People post their best pictures on social media and keep the painful ones to themselves.

A Painful Discovery

I was smack dab in the middle of another busy week between two challenging months. I had no choice except to keep pressing on, enduring, and finishing the tasks at hand. My staff was counting on me, the church needed their senior leader, and my wife would just have to understand. My three teenage children had learned how to manage with me being busy all the time. For years, even though I was physically present at home, I was emotionally absent. In my head I justified my work and promised that someday I would have the chance to make up the lost time to them.

While waiting for a flight in San Diego, I hit a wall. Actually, the wall had been there for a while, growing taller and taller until that day when I discovered I couldn't climb over it anymore. I could no longer pretend it was just another challenge to be conquered. Suddenly I found myself isolated in a very busy airport, surrounded by many people yet alone at Gate 23D.

I was solo, just me and my thoughts. I had arrived at the airport early so I could write another leadership blog, work on our church's strategic plan, and catch up on some reading. What happened next was unexpected. I began to reflect on my life and ministry. Then the waterworks turned on, right in the middle of the wrong place. Tears rolled off my cheeks, dripping onto my laptop. Normally, I would never let myself cry, but this time for some reason I couldn't stop. I have always prided myself on my ability to keep pressing ahead, to overcome issues, and tackle challenges. Yet this time I could not force myself to look ahead. In a strange way, I actually feared going home.

Suddenly, I became aware that I was wounded. I am not talking about physical wounds; I am talking about wounds inflicted in the trenches and potholes of life. These wounds had been glossed over and covered, some for years; they had never been fully dealt with. As the tears continued to flow, I decided to do something about all the pain in my life; I decided to deal with it, to let the Holy Spirit expose my wounds in order to bring healing.

It would take effort, determination, and willingness to let the Holy Spirit deal with the wounds I had spent a lifetime trying to ignore. My journey to find hope and healing started at Gate 23D. That is where I decided to do something about all the emotional pain and baggage I was carrying.

Over the next few months I dealt with seven key areas of woundedness in my life:

- ◎ The past
- ◎ Self-deception
- ◎ Fear
- ◎ Anger
- ◎ Shame
- ◎ Loss
- ◎ Unhealthy rhythms

These seven areas of wounds are not unique to me. In fact, if you allow the Holy Spirit to work in your life, you will discover that you have wounds in the same seven areas of your life as I did. The purpose of this book is to help you explore these seven areas so you can learn how to be emotionally, relationally, psychologically, and spiritually healthy. After all, isn't that what we all really want?

Over the course of two years, God healed my wounds. I want to help you experience healing as I did. And once you are healed, I want to show you how to stay healthy.

Start the Journey

How much better would your life be right now if you let God transform your wounds into something wonderful? Rather than trying to mask the wounds, what if you let Jesus redeem them and use them for his glory?

If someone tells you that once you put your faith and trust in Jesus all your problems will go away, they are wrong. If you believe that you can outwit every problem, avoid every pitfall, and solve every situation without getting wounded, you are wrong. However, God can turn your woundedness into something wonderful. God never wastes your pain. He can and will redeem it if you make the choice to stop hiding it.

I want to help you see your wounds so you can let the Holy Spirit start to heal them. I am going to push you and challenge you to go places that you may have been avoiding for years. This isn't a book about theory; it's a book that has been mined out of my own storyline along with the wise counsel and wisdom of others. The healing I have found is available to you through the power of the Holy Spirit. Jesus has been working in my wounds and has brought hope and healing I never thought possible. My prayer for you is that you will find the same hope and healing that I have. David prayed, *"Search me, God, and know my heart; test me and know my anxious thoughts. See if there is any offensive way in me, and lead me in the way everlasting,"* (Psalm 139:23-24).

As you read through the following chapters, you will be working through emotional, relational, and psychological wounds that people commonly incur and often fail to fully deal with, or even recognize. Ask the Holy Spirit to help you to connect with your emotions. Allow the Holy Spirit to work in your woundedness and allow Him to move you to a place of wonderfulness.

You may need to find a quiet place to read this book in order to connect with your emotions. When you encounter your own wounds, don't ignore them or pretend they don't exist. Be honest with yourself so you can find hope and healing from the pain that has been festering in your life for so long. Don't be afraid to cry. You might work through the book quickly, or it might take you a few weeks. You may have to go back and reread certain chapters to deal with feelings you missed the first time around. If so, that's okay and quite normal. Just keep pressing ahead.

No matter what you have gone through or how much hurt you are still harboring, God can and will help you process it, part with it, and heal from it. I know because that is what He has done for me. My specific wounds may not be the same as yours, but we are all wounded and our source of healing is the same. Healed wounds become beautiful scars that broaden your character and deepen your understanding of self and others. Healed wounds will no longer hurt; they can actually help bind you to Jesus in a profound way.

Your wounds are part of your story, but they should not define your story. You need to be the person God created you to be, and you can if you are willing to expose your woundedness and accept the wonderful healing that is available to you. I'm praying for you.

CHAPTER 1

IDENTIFY YOUR WOUNDS

A physical wound is an injury to living tissue caused by a cut, blow, or other impact, typically one in which the skin is broken. Physical wounds are treated with sutures, bandages, surgery, slings, and many other medical procedures.

But physical wounds are not the only types of wounds that exist. An emotional wound is often much more difficult to deal with than a scrape, booboo, or cut. Emotional wounds can hurt for weeks, months, years, or even decades. Emotional wounds originate from psychological or emotional trauma. A person's psyche is emotionally damaged after experiencing an extremely frightening or distressing event, and he or she may face challenges in functioning or coping normally afterward.

Inner wounds always manifest themselves externally as they are reflected in your words and actions. You may try to mask them, but they always come out. Wounds can cause powerful insecurities that manifest themselves in a number of negative ways. They may cause you to lose your temper with your spouse or kids. They keep you from being transparent with friends or from getting close to others. Your wounds are exposed when you are judgmental of others or when you gossip. Your wounds are revealed when you can never get enough money or sex or porn, when you never feel good enough or successful enough and you feel compelled to impress others all the time. Wounds can result in shame, anger, anxiety, depression, restlessness, frustration, guilt, addiction, and lack of meaning and fulfillment in life. These wounds bleed over into other areas of life, impacting your faith and ministry. Many people leave ministry because of their wounds.

Most of us press ahead, masking our wounds with work, humor, and emotional escape mechanisms such as alcohol, drugs, pornography, and binge-watching television programs. We mask our wounds by playing video games, overeating, shopping, or doing almost anything taken to an extreme. Even healthy activities or interests can become drugs used to anesthetize our wounds. People even try to mask their misery with a thin layer of hyper-spiritualism. Others mask their wounds by becoming judgmental of others, hypercritical, uncaring, distant, and disconnected. Myriads of Christians change churches in search of greener pastures and more receptive people, yet they find that all of them fall short in some area. We pretend everything is going great and tell others how blessed we are when, in reality, it is just a show.

One unknown sage noted, "We shout our glory stories and whisper our pain." How true is that? We carefully and cautiously create the image we want others to have of us. We filter, crop, and photoshop our lives through social media, always putting on our best face for the viewing public. We spend so much time trying to paint our lives the way we want others to perceive us that we become masters of disguise, hiding our true selves.

Your wounds impact what you think about yourself and what you tell yourself. When someone lashes out, it's really easy to soak it in and actually start to believe what they said. Because of something a gym teacher said to me in junior highschool, I thought I was ugly and too tall and that nobody would love me because I looked weird. I told myself this lie for years. And after a youth pastor blasted me and stormed out of the church, I started to believe what he said—that I was a terrible leader and God had left me. It sounds crazy to let other people's words wound us so much, but they can.

A wounded person who has not yet been healed might express the damage in various indirect ways. He or she might:

- Exhibit distrust of others.
- Display emotional outbursts.
- Express self-hate, self-blame, guilt or shame.
- Have low self-esteem or confidence.
- Cry easily, frequently.
- Express feelings of hopelessness.
- View death as a viable option.
- Abuse alcohol or other substances.
- Be fearful of intimacy and touch.
- Exhibit passive-aggressive behaviors.
- Obsess, worry or appear anxious about performance.
- Have difficulty sleeping.
- Become isolated from others, emotionally withdrawn, detached.
- Be fearful of abandonment and rejection.

A critical first step to admitting your woundedness is to recognize that you are not alone. Wounded people live in every corner of society, culture, business, government, education, churches, and family. Wounded people are judges, lawmakers, law enforcement officials, medical practitioners, military leaders, religious personages, teachers, and even counselors. No level of society or occupation is exempt.

And although we can sometimes see subtle hints of wounds in others, we rarely reflect on our own. When it comes to dealing with our own wounds, we wave the white flag and just give in to them, never dealing with them or working through them. Unwittingly embracing some form of denial, we put on a really good show for everyone around us.

Being wounded doesn't make you worthless or beyond repair. The Bible clearly teaches that nobody is beyond the reach of God. Therefore, everyone is capable of being redeemed and restored.

Have you dealt with your wounds or have you just learned to hide them really well? You need to know that if you don't let Christ transform your pain, you will transmit it. You will transmit it to your family, friends, coworkers, church, and community. If you want to find inner healing you are going to have to look within and get in touch with your real feelings, needs, and values.

Self-perception can be painful. Finding healing and moving from a place of woundedness to a place of wonderfulness is going to take some work. Admitting and identifying your wounds is the first step in starting to take control of the pain they have caused and are still causing. You can do this and begin to experience profound healing in the process. I am convinced, once you start to connect with your emotions, painful as it may be, you will begin to be free to write a wonderful new chapter in your life.

The Origin of Wounds

Where do wounds come from? Who or what causes them, and why do they hurt so much? We begin to feel the sting from wounds at an early age, and they originate from a variety of sources, some easily determined and others not. Some take periods of deep introspection to flush out.

Family Wounds

Family wounds hurt the most and are also the most common. There is no such thing as a perfect family, and sometimes those who are the closest to you can cause the most pain. Even if you grew up in a solid nuclear family, chances are you still have some family scarring from a parent, sibling, or extended family member.

Wounds can come from family members who say hurtful words such as: "You will never amount to anything," "You are a failure," "I wish you had never been born," or "I can't wait until you get out of here for good."

Ask yourself some questions:

- Did your family look at you in a way that made you self-conscious?
- Did your family constantly judge your performance?
- Was their love conditional, based on your performance?
- Were you emotionally neglected?
- Was religion crammed down your throat to the point you hated God?
- Did you never live up to expectations?
- Did a family member tell you that you were not wanted?
- Was your home life unstable, with male or female adults coming and going every few months or years?

Write down any family wounds you can remember.

_____

_____

_____

_____

_____

Father Wounds

If you had a dad who was always demanding more of you, it could have created a wound in your life. No matter how well you did, never being able to please Dad made an impact on you. Or your dad could have been emotionally absent in your life. (Just because your father came home every night doesn't mean he was emotionally present.)

There is no doubt that "daddy issues" impact a person's ability to relate to others on an intimate level and many people have deep wounds stemming from years of tumultuous family drama or neglect. If you had a dad who was emotionally negligent, physically absent, verbally abusive, or who abused alcohol, it probably created a wound in your life. In a conversation I had with a friend, she told me no matter how good her grades were in school or how well she performed in sports, it was never good enough for her dad. As a result, she is never pleased with her own performance as the mother of two children or with her results at the office. She said, "I am thirty-five years old and am still trying to win the approval of my father in everything I do even though he has been dead for six years." The cumulative wounds from her father still have a profound impact on her today.

Ask yourself:

- ◉ Was your father physically abusive?
- ◉ Was your father emotionally abusive?
- ◉ Was your father spiritually abusive?
- ◉ Was your father absent or uninvolved in your life?
- ◉ Did your father release his anger on you?
- ◉ Were you scared of your father?

Write down any father wounds you can remember.

_____

_____

_____

_____

_____

Mother Wounds

If your mother was judgmental or angry or unloving, it wounded you. In an article titled "8 Toxic Patterns in Mother-Daughter Relationships," author Peg Streep wrote,

> It's true enough that all daughters of unloving and unattuned mothers have common experiences. The lack of maternal warmth and validation warps their sense of self, makes them lack confidence in or be wary of close emotional connection, and shapes them in ways that are both seen and unseen.

She goes on to say that some mothers are dismissive, controlling, unavailable, or enmeshed with their children.

Other mothers are so engrossed in their own dysfunction that they are incapable of giving and receiving authentic love, which wounds their children. Self-involved mothers often go to great lengths to manage their public image, making it look as though everything in their world is amazing. At first glance, they may come across as poised and well-presented. They probably take care of their homes, juggle their work responsibilities, and attend social events. But they have insufficient emotional bonds with their kids, which makes their children feel unloved.

Consider the following questions:

- ◎ Was your mother overbearing?
- ◎ Did your mother set unrealistic or unclear expectations of you?
- ◎ Was your mother verbally or physically abusive?
- ◎ Was your mother absent from your life?
- ◎ Did your mother neglect to keep you safe?

Write down any mother wounds you can remember.

_____

_____

_____

_____

_____

Sibling Wounds

Some people have experienced painful abuse from a sibling. This abuse could be physical, emotional, or even sexual. Do you feel like "The redheaded stepchild," (a phrase commonly used to denote blatant favoritism within a family)? For example, if one sibling is highly athletic and the other is not, this can cause competition within the family for parental attention.

Take a minute to reflect on your own sibling wounds. Can

you identify any? Was there anything in particular that impacted your self-esteem in a profoundly negative way?

- ◉ Did you have an abusive sibling?
- ◉ Did your siblings tease you?
- ◉ Did your siblings ignore or abandon you?
- ◉ Did your siblings physically abuse you?
- ◉ Were you emotionally abused by your siblings?
- ◉ Were you sexually abused by your siblings or stepsiblings?

Write down any sibling wounds you can remember.

_____

_____

_____

_____

_____

Childhood Wounds

When I was only five years old, my friend and neighbor Betsy died from leukemia. I didn't understand death at the time and had no idea how to process it. No five-year-old can. Years later, when my own son was diagnosed with leukemia at age three and a half, I immediately associated it with death since Betsy was the only person I ever knew who had it and she died. An old hidden wound from a childhood loss became a fresh wound when I was an adult.

Another example: Early in elementary school my parents held me back, and I had to repeat the first grade. They made the decision because I was falling behind academically, and they made it with the best of intentions—but it had a big impact on me. I was teased relentlessly by kids who were my age but a grade higher than I was. In reaction, I bullied the kids in my grade. At a high school reunion, I ran into a woman who reminded me that I had bullied her by pulling her pants down in front of her friends in the grade school yard. All I could do was apologize and ask her to forgive me. I didn't even remember the incident, but she did, in vivid detail.

When I was a young teenager, my grandfather was diagnosed with brain cancer and suffered for a year with it. He endured radiation treatments and surgery that cost him his health. At the time, I didn't understand how to process it. I remember the pain on my parents' faces as they talked about his diminishing health and the reality that there was nothing else the doctors could do. When he died, I was crushed.

What childhood wounds have you sustained?

- Did you have a friend die?
- Were you teased?
- Did you ever wet your pants at school?
- Did something traumatic happen to you?
- Did you feel unloved by your peers?
- Were you made to feel different?

Write down any childhood wounds you can remember.

_____

_____

_____

_____

_____

_____

Adolescent Wounds

Even in the best of circumstances, adolescence is tough. Teens put relentless pressure on themselves to fit in and gain popularity. Social media has increased the awkwardness of adolescence a hundredfold. Most physical changes to a person's body happen during the teenage years. Girls turn into young women. Boy's hormones run rampant. Pants never fit just right. Shoes come and go quicker than breakfast cereal in the morning.

When I was in junior high, all of us boys were in the locker room after gym class. While we were changing out of our shorts, the gym teacher walked in, looked at me, and said in front of the whole class, "Braland, you look like a beanpole." As soon as he said it, the entire class laughed at me in my underwear, and suddenly I became self-conscious about my body. From that moment on, I saw myself as taller and skinnier than everyone. His words wounded me and trashed my self-image for years. Every time I viewed myself in the mirror, I criticized myself, replaying the painful moment over and over. I taunted myself, saying, "You are a beanpole, Braland, and you are ugly!"

In high school, I thought I was in love with a girl who wasn't in love with me. We were friends, but I wanted it to be more. I so badly wanted to take our relationship to the next level that, when it didn't happen, I felt completely rejected. To me, it felt I had lost my place in the world. Worse than feeling unloved, I felt suicidal. My friends offered the usual remedies such as drugs and alcohol, but nothing seemed to dull the pain enough. I was broken.

Some wounds come from being chosen last time after time because you were not very good at basketball, football, or band. You may remember sitting alone at the lunch table or playing by yourself when all the other kids were playing together. Did someone call you fat? Skinny? Ugly? Or "embarrassing"?

One weekend, a woman approached me after church to share that she had been sexually abused by her uncle from the age of six until she was twelve. He told her if she told anyone about what he was doing he would kill her family. So she kept silent. Later she found out that he had told the same lie to her younger sister. In silence, she carried those painful wounds from sexual abuse for sixty years! She even made her own wound worse by convincing herself that her sister's abuse happened because she didn't speak up. When she was being abused, she was a scared little girl. Now, she is a scarred adult who desperately needs to find healing from the abuse she suffered. She has carried those horrible emotions for too long.

The wounds we receive in adolescence are more powerful than those we experience later. They tend to stick with us throughout our lives because the adolescent brain is not yet fully developed. Snide comments can become defining moments that alter the trajectory of a life.

What adolescent wounds did you receive as an teen? Are any of them still hurting you? Can you relate to any of the following scenarios?

- Teased at lunch.
- Picked last for the team or got cut.
- Failed a grade.
- Not invited to a birthday party.
- Teased by a teacher.
- Laughed at by a boy or girl you cared about.
- Picked on by teammates and/or classmates.
- Made the butt of practical jokes.

- Felt different because you could not afford the right clothes.

Write down any adolescent wounds you can remember.

Adulthood Wounds

Wounds are not just relegated to our family of origin, childhood, and adolescence. Some of our deepest and most profoundly painful wounds come during adulthood. A divorce, an abusive spouse, a bankruptcy, a failing business, wayward children, or a hostile work environment can cause incredibly painful wounds. You may feel isolated. These wounds may make you skeptical of others or unable to express love or achieve physical intimacy.

After high school, I joined the United States Air Force, where I served as a police officer. I made friends quickly, and we relied on one another during work and off duty. However, after being honorably discharged at the end of my enlistment, I struggled to find friends. My story was different than everyone else's back home. I had traveled the world and, having been deployed to a hostile area, had become very self-sufficient. I just didn't see the world like my old high school friends did anymore, and I missed my military friends.

Years later, another wound was inflicted on me. As the rest

of the world chugged along at its usual speed, my world changed dramatically when I took my three-and-a-half-year-old son Josh to a local medical clinic because he was developing bruises all over his body. I could tell the doctor was fighting back tears when she said, "Don't worry, but we are going to send a sample of blood down to Children's Hospital." In my heart, I knew something was wrong, very wrong, and I suspected leukemia. Because my childhood friend had died from leukemia, I thought my son had been handed a death sentence. I wasn't angry; I was hurt. Hurting for my son, hurting for my wife, and hurting for myself. I felt let down by God. I had prayed for my son and asked God to protect him. I had expected God to grant my prayers. Now, here we were, leaving the clinic with the likelihood of a horrible diagnosis. My heart was lost in a swell of emotion.

Early the next day, we made our first trip to Children's Hospital. In eight hours, Josh's leukemia was confirmed; we had a room on the eighth floor, the intensive care cancer floor; and were being indoctrinated into a whole new world of medical terms and treatments.

I cried too hard that day to remember many details, but I do remember going to bed that night on a lounger that extended into a bed. The chair-bed was lumpy, the room was cold and very unfamiliar. My son was peacefully sleeping just down the hall after the single worst day of his life. He had undergone surgery. An allergic reaction to a medicine they gave him and it had made him violent. He looked white as a ghost and beat up like a boxer. The world would never be the same again. I was broken to the point that I could not function normally. For several months I didn't even go shopping locally because I knew I couldn't hold it together long enough to have a conversation without waterworks pouring out of my eyes.

I was desperately trying to come to grips with what was happening in my life when a friend from church invited me out to breakfast less than a week after Josh's diagnosis. Josh had just come home from the hospital. I was an emotional mess and shared the pain I was going through. My friend listened to me for a half hour. After I had shared my heart and pain with him, he leaned forward and said, "I really don't know how to tell you this, but it's your fault your son has cancer." I was stunned. He proceeded to tell me I didn't pray for my family enough in order to close spiritual doors. He said I wasn't a "spiritual enough" Christian to protect my son. I was so hurt I didn't even have the strength to reach over the table and punch him. Instead, I stood up and left the restaurant. His words hurt me so much I began to question whether or not he was right. Was it my fault? Was I a good enough Christian? I ended up seeking counseling. I was a wounded man cut by a "caring" friend.

The wounds you feel as an adult tend to stick with you longer than you think. As an adult, you unwittingly utilize all of the coping skills you have learned throughout the years. You may cope by becoming an introvert, a recluse, or a homebody. You may troll social media, although it can trigger such jealousy and anger that you say nothing to anyone. You strive for neutrality and the safety of the world you know. Rather than dating again, you would rather remain alone; the pain of being alone is at least predictable. You stay at the same job, even if you hate it, because you don't think any other company would want to hire you. So you just stay alive day after day, not really living. Deep inside you want more but are sick of being hurt, so you remain as you are, where you are.

Beyond that time of crisis, I realized that I have often felt like a failure as a husband, father, and friend. Sometimes these feelings came from the pressures to perform that I placed on myself and other times the feelings originated from the spiteful mouths and irrational e-mails of others. I have been wounded by my own sinful actions and selfish behavior—and the guilt that accompanies it.

How about you?

- Were you ever fired?
- Do you work with an abrasive coworker?
- Do people gossip about you at the office?
- Do you feel inferior to someone?
- Did your spouse cheat on you?
- Did you have a dream die?
- Did or does your spouse abuse you?
- Have you gone through a divorce?
- Did a close friend die?
- Have you lost a parent?
- Has your relationship with your child or children crumbled?
- Do you still speak to your adult child or do they speak to you?
- Have you seen your grandkids?
- Did a family member move far away?

Write down your wounds from adulthood.

_____

_____

_____

_____

_____

Self-Inflicted Wounds

Not all wounds are the direct result of others. Some of the wounds we carry, often concealed from our own awareness, come directly from the decisions we have made and the actions we have taken. Have you lost your temper with someone in public or someone close to you? Maybe you said something like, "I can't stand you, you are a waste of space," to another person, possibly even your spouse, and have regretted it ever since. Although your words wounded the recipient, they also wounded you, and now you are plagued with guilt and shame. You replay the scene over and over. Now you, consciously or subconsciously, think about it every time you see that person.

Angry outbursts reflect a troubled heart, which always indicates deeper struggles. Whenever you or I lose our temper or make a poor decision it, can cause a cut that festers.

Poor financial decisions can also cause self-inflicted wounds. The desire to fit in, to have something nice, or even to take a vacation can lead you to make bad financial decisions, which can become a form of soul poison. If you add up all of your self-inflicted wounds, it can feel like death by a thousand paper cuts.

What self-inflicted wounds do you have?

- Did you hurt someone emotionally, physically, spiritually, or sexually?
- Did you say something hurtful?
- Did you do something harmful to someone?
- Did you make a poor choice?
- Did you get into financial trouble?
- Did you hire the wrong person and regret it?
- Did you fire the wrong person and relive it?

⊚   Did you have to make painful budget cuts that tore
relationships apart?

Write down your self-inflicted wounds.

_____

_____

_____

_____

_____

Self-Bashing

A disturbing number of women confess to having a constant
stream of hateful thoughts about their own bodies. They call
themselves "fat," "ugly," "big-lipped," "pigeon-toed," and endless
other self-bashing terms. Men are similar, thinking self-accusing
thoughts such as, "You're worthless," "Nobody would ever hire
you," and "Women think you are an idiot."

We repeat what others have said to us and magnify our own
perceived shortcomings or failures. Dr. Lisa Firestone wrote,

> There are two important influences on how we form
> our self-perception. The first is how our parents or
> other early influential caretakers saw and treated us.
> The second is the way these same influential figures saw
> themselves. Parents are people; they aren't perfect. They
> both love and hate themselves, and they extend these
> reactions to their products (their children).[1]

---

1 Firestone, Lisa. "Stop Hating Yourself Once and For All." PsychAlive.
September 15, 2017. Accessed July 14, 2018. https://www.psychalive.org/stop-
hating-yourself.

All of the relentless self-bashing causes wounds to stick and fester. We don't feel like we can make any progress because we have already labeled ourselves a failure and a quitter. So before anyone else can say something negative, we jump at the chance to insult ourselves repeating what we perceive others to already be saying.

What self-bashing statements do you or have you made?

- "I am a loser."
- "I am fat."
- "I am ugly."
- "Nobody wants me."
- "I am a fool."
- "My kids hate me."
- "I'm a terrible person."
- "I am a drunk."
- "I look like such a dweeb."
- "I hate being me."

Write down the self-bashing statements you say to yourself.

_____

_____

_____

_____

_____

Ministry Wounds

Being in ministry is tough. I have been in ministry for over twenty years and have had to fight off spiritual attacks from the enemy, slander from people I thought were friends, quarrels among board members, and infighting from church members. Church leaders, elders, boards—all are made up of imperfect people, broken people, hurting people, which often makes them hurtful people, and that includes you and I. All believers bring a slice of their past into the holy calling to live out their faith.

We hired a student ministries pastor who was passionate for students and desired to help them grow closer to Christ. These qualities were attractive to us. During the interview process, someone on our team asked him why he left his past church. He explained that the pastor and elders did not handle a certain situation very well, so he quit. He didn't go into detail, and we didn't press into the matter further. It didn't take long for the cracks in his character to become exposed. He was judgmental and hyper-spiritual, excluding parents and students alike who didn't fit into his ministry mindset. Several years later, he quit and left the church, blaming me for ruining his ministry. A dozen other families also left, vocal and angry, convinced that their pastor had been victimized.

What really hurt me the most was that many of my kids' friends were friends with the majority of the people who left the church in the fallout. My kids were so hurt by what happened they were mad at me, God, our church, and this man they used to call pastor. Our entire family suffered because of the slander. The collateral damage to our family ran much deeper than I would have ever guessed.

Rather than letting his words just roll off my back, I let them echo in my head, causing more damage. For several months after his departure, I questioned my calling. I prayed about leaving the church and wondered if God had abandoned my ministry there. I felt insecure as a leader, and I became hesitant to make decisions. I started to become a people-pleaser. I didn't like going to the store because I didn't want to talk to people. Ministry is tough; I have the gray hair and wrinkles to prove it. Wounds can come from anyone and everywhere. If we are honest, we can admit that we have them and that they hurt.

Do you have any ministry wounds? What are they? Who or what caused them? Can you relate to any of the following comments?

- ◉ "You are a terrible pastor."
- ◉ "You should be fired."
- ◉ "There are a lot of us who think that..."
- ◉ "I heard people saying..."
- ◉ "Do you even try to follow God?"
- ◉ "You are not very spiritual."
- ◉ "If people knew what you get away with."
- ◉ "You have hurt me and my family."
- ◉ "You are unloving."

Write down the wounding statements about your ministry that still echo in your head.

_____

_____

_____

_____

_____

Other Sources of Wounding

- ◉ Adultery

- Negative labels
- Job loss
- Personal financial collapse
- Wayward children
- Emotional neglect
- Sexual abuse
- Rejection
- Death of someone close to you
- Difficult circumstances
- Poor decisions that resulted in substantial negative consequences
- Bad relationships
- Personal failure

Write down any wounds that the Holy Spirit is bringing to light in your life right now.

_____

_____

_____

_____

_____

_____

The Cover-Up

We smother our woundedness in busyness, addiction, and the pursuit of pleasure, and we protect ourselves from more rejection with isolation. We don't talk about the divorce, the family problems, or the pain that comes from being part of a broken family. Like mannequins elegantly dressed and staged to impress gawking shoppers, we become experts at creating false personas. We do our very best to keep our broken lives and shattered emotions hidden from others because, God forbid, someone might find out how we really feel inside. We fear being judged, labeled, or looked down on. We long to be loved and accepted with all of our warts and scars.

Good News for Wounded People

The Gospel is the story of God's willingness to be wounded in order to redeem imperfect, wounded people and use them to bless a fractured world. The beauty of salvation comes from Jesus' willingness to be wounded for us on the cross. The prophet Isaiah prophesied this about Jesus hundreds of years before He was born. Foretelling Jesus, he wrote,

> *He had no beauty or majesty to attract us to him, nothing in his appearance that we should desire him. He was despised and rejected by mankind, a man of suffering, and familiar with pain. Like one from whom people hide their faces he was despised, and we held him in low esteem. Surely he took up our pain and bore our suffering, yet we considered him punished by God, stricken by him, and afflicted. But he was pierced for our transgressions, he was crushed for our iniquities; the punishment that brought us peace was on him, and by his wounds we are healed. We all, like sheep, have gone astray, each of us has turned to our own way; and the Lord has laid on him the iniquity of us all.* (Isaiah 53:2–6)

Jesus experienced deep wounding in His life and death. He was wounded so you can be healed. You can find healing and inner peace. Jesus' broken body hung on a broken tree and that brokenness is our salvation. The Gospel message is God's tangible touch on your life. Once you admit you are wounded, you can begin the journey of healing by letting the Holy Spirit into the pain. You need to deal with your wounds or the emotional pain will clutter every decision, every relationship, and every opportunity, stopping you in your tracks from stepping into the future God has for you.

> But we have this treasure in jars of clay to show that this all-surpassing power is from God and not from us. We are hard pressed on every side, but not crushed; perplexed, but not in despair; persecuted, but not abandoned; struck down, but not destroyed. (2 Corinthians 4:7–9)

As a Christian, you have to come to the point when you have nothing left to hide. That is the moment you stop making excuses for whatever it is that happened and let God start to heal it. You need to get radically real with God, giving Him full disclosure, because it opens a door for the healing process to begin. I spent the first part of my life trying to hide and ignore my wounds. Now, I am learning how to admit them, understand them, and work through them so I can authentically praise God and live in a state of wonderful content.

The Kintsugi Concept

As you begin the process of examining your wounds, you may question if there is any hope, wondering if any love, beauty, or blessing can come from the broken pieces of what used to be your life. There have been times when I felt I was wounded beyond repair. Feeling like Humpty Dumpty, the wounds drove me to reflect on my calling as a leader and as a man. Did God really call me into ministry? Does He really want me to continue? Am I making any difference? Can I even be a good husband, father, and friend? The depression that accompanied those feelings was all too real and painful.

Kintsugi is known as "golden joinery" or "golden repair." It is the "Japanese art of repairing broken pottery with lacquer dusted or mixed with powdered gold, silver, or platinum. As a philosophy, it treats breakage and repair as part of the history of an object, rather than something to disguise."[2]

Kintsugi embraces the flaws and imperfections in pottery. The art of kintsugi actually highlights the cracks and repairs "as simply an event in the life of an object rather than the end of it."[3]

---

2 "Kintsugi," *Wikipedia* (https://en.wikipedia.org/wiki/Kintsugi), accessed June 21, 2018. See also "A Kintsugi Life: Finding the treasure in life's scars (https://akintsugilife.com/about-kintsugi).

3 Ibid.

This art form accepts change as a reality and not something to run from or discard. It embraces and recognizes the beauty of brokenness.

How would you be different tomorrow if you embraced the concept of kintsugi in your own life right now? What if you started to see your brokenness from a different perspective? If you learned to embrace it as part of your life story and faith journey...

- ...you would be emotionally happier, healthier, and content.
- ...you would find and experience the peace that you long for.
- ...you would be able to better connect relationally with others.
- ...you would not be afraid that your fear, shame, guilt, or anger would leak out at the absolute worst time.
- ...you would not be stuck in the past.
- ...you would feel emotionally vitalized.
- ...you would feel enormous freedom to be the person God has created you to be.

Jesus never rejects anyone because of their wounds. The exact opposite is true. When you bring your wounds to Jesus, He soothes them. When Jesus gave His sermon on the side of the mountain, He said: *"Blessed are the poor in spirit, for theirs is the kingdom of heaven. Blessed are those who mourn, for they will be comforted,"* (Matthew 5:3-4). Jesus blesses the broken.

Psychologist James W. Pennebaker writes that when a person is willing to make a radical confession with full disclosure, it helps the person see the event from a whole new perspective.[4]

Are you willing to see the beauty and the blessings that can come from dealing with your wounds? If not, you will continue to spend the rest of your life trying to conceal your pain, never really making much forward progress. But if you are willing to embrace the kintsugi concept in your own life, you will be able to receive Jesus' love, see the beauty in your life, and receive the blessings that can come from healing. The Gospel enables us to value and even embrace our scars, rust, dents and dings. Although we are broken, God can restore our beauty and actually bless us in the process.

And we know that in all things God works for the good of those who love him, who have been called according to his purpose. (Romans 8:28)

Let God's love fill the cracks and embrace the beautiful person Christ says you are. This is the beauty of the Gospel, the glory of second chances graciously given by God. Jesus has compassion on people who come to him as they are, without any pretense or fear of what He may think. Don't let your wounds keep you from seeking healing in Christ. Jesus loves wounded people because He sees their beauty.

There is joy that comes with healing. God doesn't want us to stay broken, He wants to make us whole again and use us for His glory. What was once shattered and shuttered can be made

---

4   James W. Pennebaker, "Does Confessing Secrets Improve Our Mental Health?" *Scientific American*, March 2016 ((https://www.scientificamerican. com/article/does-confessing-secrets-improve-our-mental-health), accessed January 13, 2017.

new again. Your life is a testimony to the world that Jesus truly transforms people and enables them to find and experience a joy-filled life. God is willing to take your wounds, heal them, and work them into something beautiful.

Jesus Christ is the Son of God, and He willingly came and died on the cross as a substitutionary atonement for our sins. In everyday terms, this means that Jesus took a bullet for you. He willingly laid down His perfect life for imperfect people like you and me so we can be united with God. It's a simple concept, really: God loves you and me so much He was willing to die so we can have a relationship with Him.

God is reaching out to you. He loves you. Even with all of your imperfections, faults, failings, and fears, He invites you to enjoy an authentic relationship with Him. This means you can be real. You can tell God how you feel, why you are sad, that you feel lonely, that you need hope, that you are scarred. With God, you can be as real as you want because God can see right past the makeup and the polished social media posts into the center of your heart. King David wrote these tender words, "*The Lord is close to the brokenhearted and saves those who are crushed in spirit,*" (Psalm 34:18).

God is reaching out to you. He loves you. Even with all of your imperfections, faults, failings, and fears, He invites you to enjoy an authentic relationship with Him.

If you are willing to be authentic and admit your woundedness, God can redeem it and use it for His glory. He used Moses, Jonah, Jeremiah, David, Peter, and Paul and He can use you too. You may be able to fool your neighbor or even your spouse into thinking you have it all together, but God sees what's really going on. The apostle Paul writes, *"There is no one righteous, not even one,"* (Romans 3:10). God sees the real you, and He values you more than you will ever know this side of heaven. It's time to start the healing process. It's time to dig deeper than you may ever have dug before. It will be painful, it will be hard, but it definitely will be worth it. You can do this! God is with you.

CHAPTER 2

FROM DECEIT *to* TRUTH

Throughout my lifetime, tensions have always been high between North Korea and pretty much the rest of the world. After the Korean War ended in the 1950s, Korea was divided. The North Korean people have been ruled by a succession of cruel dictators who are more interested in their own public image than they are in actually leading the people.

North Korea wanted to impress the rest of the world, so they embarked on an enthusiastic building program. Just across the border from South Korea, the North Koreans built Kijong-dong village. This village is clearly visible from the South Korean border. From a distance, it looks like a beautiful city full of modern apartments, clean streets, and a functional school. The North Koreans claim there are over two hundred homes filled with everything a person could want and a family would need. They even claim to have a cutting-edge hospital, staffed with qualified doctors and nurses, that is free and accessible to every citizen.

Every day, gardeners and farmers arrive on buses to tend to the flowers and fields. Lights turn on and off in the apartments at the appropriate time of day. In fact, they turn on and off at the exact same time every day because they are set to timers. Every day, the flag is raised by the soldiers in the demilitarized zone, and every night the flag is lowered. And every day at the same time the loudspeaker sings praises of their god-like leader Kim Jong-un. By all accounts, it looks and feels like a normal, healthy North Korean village. The problem is, nobody actually lives there. Kijong-dong is known internationally as "propaganda village." The village was built to deceive the South Koreans into believing North Korea is the perfect place to live. Day after day after day the North Koreans continue to run their fake city, attempting to deceive the world into believing that North Korea is the greatest place on the planet to live.

You don't have to travel to the middle of Korea to see a propaganda village. All you need to do is step out your front door or take a drive around town. Propaganda village exists in neighborhoods and homes near you. It may even exist right in the middle of your own heart.

People have become really good at deceiving others. They present themselves to others in the way they think others would approve of, in a way they believe is most acceptable, or even in such a way they believe would give them an edge. People deceive others in an attempt to fool them into thinking they are something that they are not. "University of Massachusetts psychologist Robert Feldman has studied lying for more than a decade, and his research has reached some startling conclusions. Most shocking is that

60% of people lie during a typical 10-minute conversation and that they average two to three lies during that short timeframe."[5]

People want to portray the idyllic family. They manicure their yards, wash their cars, and even stage the front room facing the street with nice furniture. They put on makeup, buy things they cannot afford, and post amazing pictures on social media pretending that everything in their world is just great.

People are reluctant to talk about marriage problems, sexual identity issues, loneliness, addictions, and other issues for fear that they will tarnish their reputation and taint their public image. And when it comes to their kids, people are as proud as can be as long as nobody gets too personal and begins to figure out that their family has tensions and troubles.

Self-Deception

The sad reality is not only do people lie to one another, they lie to themselves. We desperately want to be defined by our trophies, not our trash. We cover physical wounds from abuse with makeup, clothing, and accessories. We cover emotional wounds with embellished stories, laughter, and arrogance. We cover relational wounds with isolation and unavailability. We cover spiritual wounds with empty rituals, doubting faith, judgment, or self-righteousness.

Wounded people say damaging words to themselves and think cutting thoughts. Phrases such as "Nobody likes you," "You are an idiot," and "You deserve the pain you are going through," are often recited over and over to oneself. These damaging words

---

5   Travis Bradberry, "Sixty Percent of Your Colleagues Are Lying to You," *Huffington Post*, February 14, 2016 (https://www.huffingtonpost.com/dr-travis-bradberry/sixty-percent-of-your-col_b_9044758.html), accessed July 17, 2018.

and cutting thoughts are false and must be recognized as such. The road from wounded to wonderful includes taking an honest assessment of the lies you tell yourself.

Think back over the words that you repeat to yourself when you look in the mirror or when you are all alone. Are there lies or half-truths that you tell yourself? Do you know what they are? What hurtful words are you repeating to yourself?

The lies you tell yourself echo in your head on either a conscious or subconscious level, and they impact everything. In a previous chapter, I shared that a gym teacher in junior high labeled me a beanpole, and I repeated those hurtful words to myself until I believed them. The lie I told myself is that I looked weird and everybody was laughing at me. For one entire summer, I didn't wear shorts because I wanted to hide my legs. I wore baggy shirts to cover my skinny arms. I was ashamed of the way I looked, and it all originated with a snide comment from someone I respected. He had no idea of the impact his words would have on my life; the fire of lies burned in my heart for years. Looking back, I don't think he even meant them to hurt, but I gave his comments space in my heart and they blossomed into an ugly, overgrown lie that I repeated over and over and over.

As I mentioned in the previous chapter, somebody in my church didn't like a decision I had made, and that person became a vocal critic. Rather than letting his words of criticism roll off my, back I let them echo in my head, repeating them back to myself in the mirror and when I was alone with my thoughts. This caused me to feel insecure as a leader. I was hesitant to make decisions and started to become a people-pleaser. Subconsciously, I was trying to win him over even though he wasn't even a part of my life anymore. The lie I was telling myself is that I wasn't following God and not a good enough leader to lead a church, and I slapped myself daily with verbal insults to prove it.

Think about it for a minute. What lies have you let echo in your head or roll off your tongue? Do you even realize they are lies? What do you keep telling yourself? This can get painful because the lies you tell yourself originate from past hurts, failures, or persons. They may have originated fairly recently or back in childhood or adolescence.

Blogger Cole Schafer writes, "Our lives become the stories we tell ourselves so it's important that we are telling ourselves the right stories. If we tell ourselves lies, we create lives that don't feel true to us."[6] When you chain yourself to the past, it will disengage you from the present and keep you from stepping into a better future tomorrow.

What is the biggest lie you tell yourself? If you know what it is, circle it or write it down:

- Nobody will love me.
- I will never amount to anything.
- Nobody wants to be around me.
- I am lazy.
- I can't do anything right.
- I'll do it tomorrow.
- I am fat.
- I am ugly.
- I am dumb.
- I should stop caring.
- I should stop trying.
- I am a loser.

6   Cole Schafer, "The lies we tell ourselves," February 28, 2018 (http://coleschafer.com/blog/2018/2/28/the-lies-we-tell-ourselves), accessed July 18, 2018).

- I am a dork.
- I am a bad father.
- I am a bad mother.
- I am a nasty person.
- I am weird.
- I can't do anything right.
- It's all my fault.
- I didn't do anything wrong.
- My past will always affect me.
- Life isn't worth living.
- There is nothing I can do about it anyway.
- When I get X then everything will change.
- Other _____
- Other _____
- Other _____

Masks

Once you have identified your wound or wounds, the next step is to figure out the mask you wear to cover your wound. We wear masks to protect ourselves from scrutiny and judgment and to keep up our public image.

Examples of the masks people wear to cover their wounds:

- The "hero" mask. People who wear the hero mask embellish their stories just a little bit all the time to make themselves look like the hero of the story, no matter what story they tell. They think that popularity equates to value. This mask covers insecurity.
- The "martyr" mask. People who wear this mask are always boasting about how much they do for everyone else. They will tell you they are the ones who are always

sacrificing, always going the extra mile, always doing more than their fair share, and they want everyone else to know it. This mask covers narcissism.

⊙ The "pacifist" mask. People who wear this mask pretend nothing really bothers them. People who wear this mask are usually emotionally numb or distant and come across as cold. This mask covers a deep hurt or emotional loss in the past.

⊙ The "uber-successful" mask. If you have ever gone to a class reunion, you know who wears this one. People who wear this mask want others to envy them. This mask covers depression. It may also be worn to cover insecurity.

⊙ The "yes-man" mask. People who wear this mask are always trying to please others, depleting their own emotions and mental health in the process. This mask covers relational wounds caused from interpersonal conflict.

⊙ The "I don't need anybody" mask. People who wear this mask come across as distant; they act fiercely independent. This mask covers abuse. The abuse could be physical, emotional, or even spiritual. It may have happened recently or decades ago.

⊙ The "joker" mask. The joker mask is worn by people who feel a need to be loved and accepted. This mask covers depression and/or social anxiety.

⊙ The "critical" mask. This mask is worn by people who have felt judged and now want to protect themselves from feeling judged again. This mask covers the pain caused from never feeling good enough.

⊙ The "influence" mask. This mask is birthed out of the lie that your life worth is based on your net worth. This mask covers identity issues.

- The "sarcastic" mask. This mask covers insecurity at a deep level that could have originated when a person was a child or adolescent.
- The "know it all" mask. People who wear this mask are always trying to win others over with their knowledge. This mask is worn by people who feel inferior. They have concluded that they have to prove they are not dumb.
- The "holier than thou" mask. This mask is worn by people who grew up in a legalistic home or who sat under a legalistic teaching. They don't think they are good enough but arrogantly claim to be better than others. This mask covers spiritual insecurity.

I have masked my wounds with the "hero" mask, the "yes-man" mask and the "joker" mask. I have worn these masks to cover many wounds. I have come across as arrogant, funny, insincere, and task-oriented. My own insecurities caused me to neglect my own family and friends. At times, I have been short-tempered and easily frustrated with those I worked with. I have let my critic's standards determine my standards and tamper with my identity. This made me feel miserable.

Jenny shared that no matter what she did it was never good enough for Dad. If she got a B, her dad said she could have gotten and an A if she would have tried harder. If she scored a goal, he said she could have gotten two if she would have tried harder. No matter what she did, it was never good enough for Dad. And his criticism of her caused a deep wound that she masked by being critical of others. She criticized her friends for how they raised their kids and criticized her neighbor's yard, dog, clothes, car, and everything else. She masked her wound with criticism of others, and she didn't even realize it until she was 45 years old. Then, for the first time in her life, her father told her that he was proud of her. When he said that, she cried for three days, at last realizing how much of an impact his words had on her life. Once she realized she had been telling herself the lie that she wasn't good enough, she could understand how she had masked it with criticism.

Jesus wants us to drop the masks. The mask you wear covers the lie you tell yourself, and may be enough to fool yourself and others into thinking everything is great for you, but it's not fooling God. God sees right through our masks and wants us to be real with Him. God isn't impressed with anything except honesty. So let's get honest with God and ourselves so we can let Him work on our wounds.

What mask do you wear to cover your wound? If you know it, write it down.

Truth

Once you have identified the lie you tell yourself and the mask you wear to cover it, the next step is to replace the lie with the truth. What is the truth that you need to tell yourself?

Satan wants you to believe the lies that you have been telling yourself. He wants your wounds to fester. He wants you to believe the words of death that others have spoken to you. He wants you to believe that you are not good enough or smart enough or tall enough or short enough or old enough. But Satan's lies should never trump God's truth.

Once I realized that I was wounded, it became clear that I had turned up my critic's voices and turned down God's. I had to confess my hurt to God and claim His promise that I am loved and accepted by Him. I had to take off the "yes-man" mask and stop trying to win everyone over. I had subconsciously let other people's opinions of me dictate my priorities. I worked so much that my health suffered, my relationships suffered, and my family suffered. I was a wreck and didn't even realize it until I reflected on the driving forces in my life.

God's truths found in Scripture will help heal your wounds. You need to claim them for your own life now in order to combat the lies that have taken you captive and caused so much hurt.

LIE: I am unworthy.

TRUTH: I am worthy.

"You were dead because of your sins and because your sinful nature was not yet cut away. Then God made you alive with Christ, for he forgave all our sins," (Colossians 2:13, NLT).

LIE: I am all alone.

TRUTH: I am never alone.

"Be strong and courageous. Do not be afraid or terrified because of them, for the Lord your God goes with you; he will never leave you nor forsake you," (Deuteronomy 31:6).

LIE: I am a failure.

TRUTH: I may have failed, but am not a failure.

"We are hard pressed on every side, but not crushed; perplexed, but not in despair," (2 Corinthians 4:8. See also Philippians 4:13; 1 Corinthians 15:54–57; 1 John 5:4).

LIE: I am dumb.

TRUTH: I have the mind of Christ.

"'Who can know the Lord's thoughts? Who knows

enough to teach him?' But we understand these things, for we have the mind of Christ," (1 Corinthians 2:16, NLT).

LIE: I am hopeless.

TRUTH: I have hope.

"I pray that God, the source of hope, will fill you completely with joy and peace because you trust in Him. Then you will overflow with confident hope through the power of the Holy Spirit," (Romans 15:13, NLT).

LIE: I am not good enough for God.

TRUTH: Christ died and was raised to life for me.

"But God demonstrates his own love for us in this: While we were still sinners, Christ died for us," (Romans 5:8).

LIE: I am not special.

TRUTH: I am special.

"You made all the delicate, inner parts of my body and knit me together in my mother's womb. Thank you for making me so wonderfully complex! Your workmanship is marvelous—how well I know it," (Psalm 139:13–14, NLT).

LIE: If I only had X then I would be happy.

TRUTH: I lack nothing.

"And this same God who takes care of me will supply all your needs from His glorious riches, which have been given to us in Christ Jesus," (Philippians 4:19, NLT).

LIE: I am afraid to do X.

TRUTH: I have nothing to fear.

"I prayed to the Lord and he answered me. He freed me from all my fears," (Psalm 34:4, NLT).

LIE: God will never answer my prayer.

TRUTH: God will hear my prayer and meet my needs.

"Keep on asking, and you will receive what you ask for. Keep on seeking, and you will find. Keep on knocking, and the door will be opened to you. For everyone who asks, receives. Everyone who seeks, finds. And to everyone who knocks, the door will be opened," (Matthew 7:7–8, NLT).

LIE: I am weak.

TRUTH: Christ gives me strength.

"For I can do everything through Christ, who gives me strength," (Philippians 4:13, NLT).

LIE: I am defeated.

TRUTH: I am victorious.

"No, despite all these things, overwhelming victory is ours through Christ, who loved us," (Romans 8:37, NLT).

LIE: I will always be an addict.

TRUTH: I have been set free.

"For the Lord is the Spirit, and wherever the Spirit of the Lord is, there is freedom," (2 Corinthians 3:17).

LIE: I will always be miserable.

TRUTH: I have God's comfort.

"For the Lord your God is living among you. He is a mighty savior. He will take delight in you with gladness. With his love, he will calm all your fears. He will rejoice over you with joyful songs," (Zephaniah 3:17, NLT). See also Psalm 16:11; Psalm 63:7

LIE: No one loves me.

TRUTH: I am loved by God.

> *"I have loved you even as the Father has loved me. Remain in my love,"* (John 15:9, NLT).

LIE: I don't belong.

TRUTH: I am a child of God and belong to Him.

> *"God decided in advance to adopt us into his own family by bringing us to himself through Jesus Christ. This is what he wanted to do, and it gave him great pleasure,"* (Ephesians 1:5, NLT).

LIE: I am condemned.

TRUTH: I am forgiven.

> *"So now there is no condemnation for those who belong to Christ Jesus,"* (Romans 8:1, NLT).

LIE: I cannot change.

TRUTH: I can change.

> *"So Christ has truly set us free. Now make sure that you stay free, and don't get tied up again in slavery to the law,"* (Galatians 5:1, NLT).

LIE: I have no purpose.

TRUTH: God has plans and a purpose for me.

> *"'For I know the plans I have for you,' says the Lord. 'They are plans for good and not for disaster, to give you a future and a hope,'"* (Jeremiah 29:11, NLT).

LIE: I am not needed.

TRUTH: I am needed.

> *"All of you together are Christ's body, and each of you is a part of it,"* (1 Corinthians 12:27, NLT). See also 1 Corinthians 12:18–21.

Additional truths:

- I am loved. (1 John 3:3)
- I am accepted. (Ephesians 1:6)
- I am a child of God. (John 1:12)
- I am Jesus' friend. (John 15:14)
- I am a temple of God. His Spirit and His life live in me. (1 Corinthians 6:19)
- I am a member of Christ's body. (1 Corinthians 12:27)
- I am a saint. (Ephesians 1:1)
- I am redeemed and forgiven. (Colossians 1:14)
- I am complete in Jesus Christ. (Colossians 2:10)
- I am free from condemnation. (Romans 8:1)
- I am a new creation because I am in Christ. (2 Corinthians 5:17)

Jesus wants you to take off the mask and set it at the foot of the cross. One of the biggest problems Jesus had with the Pharisees was they were fake. They were experts at living a lie. Jesus said,

Woe to you, teachers of the law and Pharisees, you hypocrites! You are like whitewashed tombs, which look beautiful on the outside but on the inside are full of the bones of the dead and everything unclean. In the same way, on the outside you appear to people as righteous but on the inside you are full of hypocrisy and wickedness. (Matthew 23:27–28)

Jesus described the Pharisees as hypocrites. In ancient literature the word hypocrite means "actor." The Pharisees were acting as though they had it all together; they wore masks to cover their own insecurities. The process of moving from wounded to wonderful begins by replacing the lies we tell ourselves with God's truth. Jesus says that the truth will set us free. *"Then you will know the truth, and the truth will set you free,"* (John 8:32).

Stop the lies. Take off the mask. Claim God's truths over your life.

Now you need to do some work. Be honest and start the process. What truth do you need to tell yourself? I am what?

Take a blank sheet of paper and write out the lie you tell yourself on one side and then flip it over and write out God's truth on the other. Take the piece of paper and tape or pin it up in a place that you will see it often, such as the bathroom mirror or refrigerator. Display it in such a way that God's truth is facing you when you look at it. This simple act will help retrain your brain to speak truth to yourself instead of the lies you have come to believe.

This is the first step in letting God heal your wound and turn it into something wonderful. God wants to meet you in your pain. He loves the real you. So drop the mask and claim the truth over your life. Once you remove the lie you have been deceiving yourself with and replace it with God's truth, you will start to see some very real rewards.

Real rewards

1. Authentic, meaningful relationships. When you remove the mask, people start to see the real you. If others aren't seeing the real you, they can only direct their emotions and affections at the person you project yourself to be and not your genuine self. Being less than authentic with others means that you will never feel truly loved for who you really are, and that's incredibly sad.

2. You attract the "right" people into your life. Because people see the real you, they will be attracted to the real you. This means you will be able to attract the right people into your life because they accept you for who you are. The people that appreciate your personality, opinions, and company will stick with you. The people that don't like the real you will exit your life, and that's not a bad thing.

3. Less worry. When you stop trying to impress others, you don't have to worry whether or not they will like you. This means you will have less relational stress and more contentment.

4. Inner peace. Being authentic and accepting yourself as you are brings inner peace. When you release your true self, you feel free to follow your passions, interests, and relationships because you are confident and comfortable in your own skin.[7]

The only way you will become the authentic person that God wants you to be is to take off the mask and claim God's truth for your life. No more hiding, no more lies. You don't have to live in propaganda village anymore. Dealing with the lies you tell yourself is just the start, so don't stop here. Take each step one at a time and let the healing love and grace of God start to soothe the wounds that have lingered in you for who knows how long. The process of moving from wounded to wonderful will take time and effort, but you can do it. God is with you and wants you to move into your next chapter in life.

---

7   See "5 Benefits of Being Authentic," Tri-Peaks Life Coaching, May 14, 2014 (http://tripeaksconsulting.com/5-benefits-of-being-authentic), accessed October 26, 2017.

CHAPTER 3

FEAR

Emotional wounds are part of everybody's story. You have them, I have them, your friends have them, and the strangers at the supermarket have them. We don't really want them; they just come from living in a broken world full of broken people. The good news is even though you have wounds, you are not powerless to heal from them. You can and you will if you choose to let the Holy Spirit seep into them.

One painful and elusive wound is fear. Fear in a person's life takes on a variety of shapes and forms. Fear can hide in your past, lurk in your present, and keep you scared about tomorrow. Fear is what makes you think twice about calling a friend when you need a friend. Fear keeps you from telling the truth to yourself and others because you are so worried they won't like you or will abandon you.

What Is Fear?

Dictionary.com defines fear as "a distressing emotion aroused by an impending danger, evil, pain, etc., whether the threat is real or imagined; the feeling or condition of being afraid." Real fear is a normal response to impending danger. If a car suddenly swerves into your lane or a dog is attempting to bite you, you should feel fear because you are in imminent danger.

Fear can be uncomfortable and crippling, but fear can also be healthy. Eliminating all fear would be the equivalent of removing all the smoke alarms in your house or the warning lights on your car dashboard because you don't like how they look and sound. Fear is a vital response to physical and emotional danger; we need it. If you don't feel fear, you cannot protect yourself from legitimate threats.

"Anxiety" is one of the many synonyms for fear. Anxiety is a general term that incorporates a wide range of emotions such as worry, apprehension, and uneasiness. More intense anxiety results in feelings of dread, distress, and panic. Fear and anxiety are often melded together and thought of as one and the same.

The word "fear" is used over five hundred times in the Bible in its various forms. The Bible describes two types of fear. The first type is human fear. Human fear is a reaction to a real or perceived threat of danger. The fear that compels you to avoid a rattlesnake or barking dog is a normal reaction to a potential danger and prepares your body to react quickly if you need to escape.

"Healthy" anxiety can be managed and reduced as the circumstances change. Actresses, actors, and athletes can learn to leverage and harness their anxiety ("the butterflies") to draw out their best performance. Anxiety can give you the burst of energy you need to meet new challenges and do your best.

The second type of fear found in the Bible is the fear of God. To fear God implies awe and profound reverence toward Him. This fear is one of reverential trust and confidence. Having a healthy fear of God means you revere, respect, and honor Him as Creator and Lord. Jesus said, "*I tell you, my friends, do not be afraid of those who kill the body and after that can do no more. But I will show you whom you should fear: Fear him who, after the killing of the body, has power to throw you into hell,*" (Luke 12:4-5). When you fear God, you elevate Him to the position of respect He is worthy of because He is Lord. Living in a constant state of human fear is debilitating, but fearing God vanquishes human fear. Thomas à Kempis said, "Fear God, and thou shalt not shrink from the terrors of men."[8]

Understanding Fear

Not all fear is real or imminent, some is imagined and perceived without the presence of any real threat. Imagined fear is a destructive emotion because the threat of pain, danger, or evil is only a false perception. We need to eradicate imagined fear from our lives.

I was too young to see the horror film *Friday the 13th* in the theater, but I did view it several years later at my cousin's house. That movie literally changed my perception of the outdoor camping scene. For years, whenever I went camping or to a cabin in the woods, my mind would drift back to certain scenes in that movie. I remembered with vivid clarity the killer named Jason jumping out of the water to grab a boater. I would look into the dark woods wondering who was out there watching me. On

---

8   Thomas à Kempis, *Of the Imitation of Christ* (15th-century classic book), chap. XXXVI.

occasion to this day some of the scenes from such movies, seen years ago, still rise up out of my subconscious memory. Why is this?

Our reaction to fear is part natural instinct, part learned, and part taught. Fear stems from a chain reaction in the brain. As soon as you experience a frightening stimulus, your body reacts to it in an effort to protect you from the danger. It works like this: Something frightens you, like hearing a door slam in an empty house, seeing a dark shadow in the woods, or a bat flying near you. As soon as you experience the frightening stimulus, a sense of panic, dread, intense anxiety, or a mix of all three comes over you. You also have physical reactions to the stimulus. Your heart pounds in your chest, your breathing quickens, your muscles tense, your stomach tenses, and you may feel like vomiting. With all of your senses heightened, your body is prepared to determine a course of action.

According to science reporter Laurie Vazquez:

> There are two different paths the fear reaction can take: the low road or the high road. The low road is the quickest, basest, least-rational response to life-threatening situations. If one of those signals is life-threatening, like feeling a knife at your throat, the thalamus alerts your amygdala. Your amygdala triggers emotional responses and prompts your hypothalamus to turn up your adrenal glands and rush blood to your muscles to get you away from the danger. If the signal isn't life-threatening, the brain takes the more rational high road response. If you see something that's not life-threatening but still frightening, like a giant spider sneaking down a wall close to you, the amygdala alerts

the pre-frontal or sensory cortex. The cortex alerts the hippocampus and spurs it to compare the current threat to past ones. The hippocampus is the brain's memory center. If it determines that the current fear stimulus is a threat but not life-threatening, the hippocampus heightens your senses to an almost superhuman degree and triggers your fight-or-flight response. Both processes are automatic and happen within "fractions of a second."[9]

The speed and thoroughness of the brain's ability to process a frightening stimulus can be detrimental. When a person experiences intense fear, the brain takes a snapshot of everything surrounding the stimulus—the time of day, images, smells, sounds, the weather, people, even the smell of their breath and posture, storing them in their long term memory. This is called "fear conditioning."[10]

The memory may be vivid and clear, but it can also be fragmented. A fragmented memory triggers all of the emotional and physical responses whenever a similar situation occurs, whether it is real or perceived. Because the stimuli were associated with some previous threat of danger or actual danger, the brain may see them as a predictor and fire off the alarms, causing one of four basic reactions to fear: Freeze, fight, flight, or fright.

The Freeze Reaction

The freeze reaction causes one to immediately stop what they are doing and focus on the source of fear in an effort to

---

9   Laurie Vasquez, "What fear does to your brain—and how to stop it," on Big Think, July 31, 2016 (https://bigthink.com/laurie-vazquez/what-fear-does-to-your-brain-and-how-to-stop-it), accessed July 3 2018).

10   Julia Layton, "How Fear Works," How Stuff Works (https://science.howstuffworks.com/life/inside-the-mind/emotions/fear4.htm), accessed October 27, 2018.

decide what to do next. The freeze reaction makes seconds seem like hours. Someone experiencing the freeze, reaction may be startled by a lurking shadow or suspicious noise and immediately freeze, focusing all of their attention on the threat in an effort to determine their next course of action.

The Fight Reaction

Your brain quickly determines if you need to defend yourself against the threat and fight it or flee from it. If your brain determines to fight the threat, your adrenaline works double-time and you will do whatever you can to neutralize the threat. You don't think about how you will fight the threat, you just do it.

The Flight Reaction

If you brain determines you need to get away from the threat, you will do whatever it takes to get as far away from the threat as fast as possible. People in flight mode are only focused on getting away.

The Fright Reaction

When the fear is overwhelming, you experience fright. You don't do anything except obsess about the shadow, the layoffs, the person, or the dreadful possibilities, whether or not they are real or perceived. Being continuously in a state of fright is an indicator you are experiencing chronic fear.[11]

Chronic Fear

Everyone feels fearful at times. Fear is part of our emotional

---

11   Adapted from "7 Things You Need to Know About Fear," *Psychology Today*, November 19, 2015 (https://www.psychologytoday.com/us/blog/smashing-the-brainblocks/201511/7-things-you-need-know-about-fear), accessed July 3, 2018.

chemistry; God hard-wired it into our lives. But temporary fear is one thing and chronic fear is another. Chronic fear is often imagined or perceived fear that has taken up residence in a person's psyche. Those with chronic fear typically struggle to regulate their emotions or read nonverbal cues clearly; they may be unable to thoroughly think through the stimulus before reacting to it. Chronic fear has far-reaching effects that can keep a person locked in a cage of perpetual insecurity.

Consequences of Living With Chronic Fear

Living with chronic fear has serious health consequences. According to health writer Erin Monahan,

> Your body is designed to react quickly to fear, sending out powerful hormones and signals to various body systems to give you the energy to run or the power to fight. In some people, the fear impulse goes awry, and coping mechanisms become unmanageable, resulting in a disorder that causes the body to feel the side effects of fear even when there is nothing to fear. However, even when no anxiety disorder is present, these processes will cause unpleasant physical side effects as your body works in survival mode.[12]

It is important to understand the consequences of living with chronic fear so that you can accurately diagnose its presence in your life.

Physical Health

Chronic fear weakens one's immune system and can cause

---

12   Erin Monahan, "What Are the Physical Side Effects of Fear?" Livestrong, (https://www.livestrong.com/article/284098-what-are-the-physical-side-effects-of-fear), accessed July 20, 2018.

cardiovascular damage, decreased fertility, and gastrointestinal problems such as ulcers and irritable bowel syndrome. It can lead to accelerated ageing and even premature death.[13]

Memory

Chronic fear can impair formation of long-term memories and cause damage to certain parts of the brain, such as the hippocampus. This can make it even more difficult to regulate fear and can leave a person anxious most of the time.

Mental Health

Fear can interrupt processes in our brains that regulate emotions and interpret nonverbal cues and other information presented to us, processes that enable us to act ethically and to reflect before acting. This impacts our thinking and decision-making in negative ways, leaving us susceptible to intense emotions and impulsive reactions. Fear can also create indecisiveness that results in stagnation. All of these side effects of fear can leave us unable to act appropriately. Consequences of chronic fear include fatigue, clinical depression, and PSTD.[14] Fear may also lead to destructive habits. In an effort to numb chronic fear, some people turn to drugs, alcohol, or binge-watching TV as a means of escape.

Fear steals your peace, robs your life of contentment, and keeps you from experiencing joy. When you are constantly afraid, your primary focus is always negative, pessimistic, and gloomy.

---

13   See Jaime Rosenberg, "The Effects of Chronic Fear on a Person's Health," paper presented at the 2017 Congress of the Neuroscience Education Institute (NEI), published November 11, 2017 (https://www.ajmc.com/conferences/nei-2017/the-effects-of-chronic-fear-on-a-persons-health), accessed October 27, 2018.

14   "The Impact of Fear and Anxiety," University of Minnesota (https://www.takingcharge.csh.umn.edu/enhance-your-wellbeing/security/facing-fear/impact-fear), accessed October 27, 2018.

Physical Weakness

Those who suffer from chronic fear often feel physically weak. They may be unable to move or move in a jittery fashion with wobbly knees. Weakness caused by chronic fear is typically a "fright" response causing your body to "play dead" in an effort to make it unappetizing to a predator. Weakness is typically the last response to fear after your body has deemed freezing, fighting, or fleeing ineffective.

Relational Damage

Chronic fear can act as a roadblock keeping a person from engaging with others in meaningful relationships or even going out in public. You can't get close to people if you are afraid they will hurt you or abandon you. If you are chronically fearful, you won't trust others or love them because your fear always stands like a brick wall between you and others.

Spiritual Health

Chronic fear has a profound impact on a person's spiritual health. No one can live the abundant life when they feel chained to a fear-inducing stimulus or situation. Chronic fear alters a person's perception of God and causes a multitude of problems. Some of the potential consequences of chronic fear on a person's spiritual health include the following:

- ◎ Bitterness toward God or others
- ◎ Confusion about or disgust with God or religion
- ◎ Loss of trust in God and/or members of the clergy
- ◎ Immobility: waiting for God to fix it
- ◎ Despair related to a perceived loss of spirituality[15]

---

15 Rosenberg, Jamie. "The Effects of Chronic Fear on a Person's Health." AJMC. November 11, 2017. Accessed October 27, 2018. https://www.ajmc.com/conferences/nei-2017/the-effects-of-chronic-fear-on-a-persons-health.

There will always be moments in life when we have doubts and fear. There will be times when we struggle to trust God. We will have fears, but they don't have to confine us or define us.

Fear in the Bible

The Bible is filled with stories about real people who felt fear, for example, Gideon. When God first commanded him to rescue the Israelites, Gideon was hiding from his enemies in a winepress (see Judges 6:11). Gideon's fear, anxiety, and doubt drove him to test God, asking Him to perform a number of signs.[16] Intensely fearful, Gideon tested God to see if He really meant what He had said. When at length, he decided to fully trust God and obey His calling, the Israelites were freed from seven years of oppression.

Throughout the Bible, we see how Satan and his demons seek to harm people, and fear can also result from demonic attack. Satan is cunning and capable of leveraging fear to cause harm. He wants to smother people with fear so they feel helpless and isolated. Believers are advised to *"be alert and of sober mind. Your enemy the devil prowls around like a roaring lion looking for someone to devour,"* (1 Peter 5:8). Satan uses fear to lure you away from God; he tempts you to rely on your own resources. The Bible clearly says that Christians are able to resist the devil and flee from him. *"Submit yourselves, then, to God. Resist the devil, and he will flee from you,"* (James 4:7).

Satan wants you to live in fear and to be ineffective. He wants to keep you isolated and in bondage. It is foolish to underestimate his cunning ability to deceive and harm you, and it is equally foolish to believe that you cannot resist the devil's attacks.

---

16 First he asked God to consume an offering of food he presented to the angel (Judges 6:20–21). Then he petitioned God to allow the morning dew to fall only on a piece of fleece he laid out, asking Him to do the exact opposite the next day (Judges 6:37–40).

You can combat the fear-producing attacks of the enemy with God's truth. One way you can look at it is to put on the "full armor of God."

> *Finally, be strong in the Lord and in his mighty power. Put on the full armor of God, so that you can take your stand against the devil's schemes. For our struggle is not against flesh and blood, but against the rulers, against the authorities, against the powers of this dark world and against the spiritual forces of evil in the heavenly realms. Therefore put on the full armor of God, so that when the day of evil comes, you may be able to stand your ground, and after you have done everything, to stand. Stand firm then, with the belt of truth buckled around your waist, with the breastplate of righteousness in place, and with your feet fitted with the readiness that comes from the gospel of peace. In addition to all this, take up the shield of faith, with which you can extinguish all the flaming arrows of the evil one. Take the helmet of salvation and the sword of the Spirit, which is the word of God. And pray in the Spirit on all occasions with all kinds of prayers and requests. With this in mind, be alert and always keep on praying for all the Lord's people.* (Ephesians 6:10–18)

Freedom From Chronic Fear

You don't have to live with chronic, debilitating fear; there is hope. God wants you to be set free from fear and will help you get free from its grip. Overcoming fear is a three-step process. When you learn and practice these three steps, you can break the cycle of fear.

STEP 1: NAME YOUR FEARS.

Everyone has fears, some are real while others are imagined or perceived. What do you fear?

- Losing your job
- Not being able to provide for family
- Being alone
- Dying
- Losing a loved one
- The future
- Divorce
- Failing
- Telling someone the truth
- Telling someone you love him/her
- How others may respond if you share your true emotions
- Being labeled
- Being teased
- Being a bad parent
- Losing your temper
- Looking different
- Rejection
- Stop self-medicating
- Letting God down
- Trying something new
- That your past will come up
- Being judged by others
- Not being good enough
- Being laughed at
- Being poor
- Making a bad investment
- Not finishing

- Getting sick
- Vomiting
- Growing old

Make a list of the things that cause you to be fearful. Rank them in order of severity. This is the first step in overcoming fear.

Now go back through your list and underline, circle, or highlight the fears that are only perceived or imaginary fears. These are the fears that are born from irrational thinking. Irrational thinking translates into lies such as:

- "I can't tell them how I really feel because then they will judge me and hate me, and I won't be able to go on."
- "Everyone will hate my idea."
- "She will laugh at me, and I'll feel like a fool."
- "I am a failure."
- "I am all alone. Nobody cares about what I am going through, so why mention it?"

Do you create negative mental scenarios and repeat them to yourself over and over, convincing yourself that your perceptions are true or will come true? You may feel afraid, unsettled, worried, and anxious for no apparent reason. This is irrational thinking and often leads to chronic fear. This is what you need to eradicate from your life. Don't give it free rein in your life.

When you feel fear, what irrational thoughts do you have? Write them down.

STEP 2: CONFRONT FEAR WITH TRUTH.

The second step is to confront the irrational fear with truth. What are you telling yourself when you feel fear? Are you telling yourself the truth? Do your thoughts line up with reality? Do they line up with Scripture? Challenge your irrational thoughts, reformulating them to reflect reality. We all conduct a continuous internal dialogue with ourselves. This self-talk greatly affects our emotions, behaviors, and responses. When we start telling ourselves lies that don't line up with reality, or that contradict Scripture, fear sets in. These misperceptions are a playground for Satan and can magnify a threat of danger beyond reality or create an imaginary threat that feels real.

Apply Rational Thinking

You combat irrational thinking with rational thinking. This is done by taking the mental high road, rethinking the fear in context. You don't have to automatically react to a stimulus the same way every time. You can take your thoughts captive and apply rational thinking. Rational thinking translates into true statements and thoughts that will eliminate or minimize the chronic fear.

Examples of rational thoughts:

- "I am going to tell them how I really feel because my thoughts are important. If they don't like the way I feel, it will be awkward but life will still go on."
- "Other people do care about me, I don't have to isolate myself."
- "What other options do I need to consider?"

One of my greatest fears was the fear of failure. I was afraid of failing as a pastor, husband, father, and friend. I replayed scenarios in my head of things not working out: my church firing me, my friends walking away from me, my kids telling me that I was a terrible dad. My thoughts turned into an irrational dialogue in my head that I played over and over for weeks at a time. The fear of failure kept me from enjoying moments of triumph and celebrating milestones. This fear of failure didn't go away after a month or two; it lasted for years and jumped out at the most inappropriate times. I never would have said I had given the fear of failure free rein in my life, but I had. I gave it free rein because I never confronted it with the truth.

Rational thinking involves speaking truth to yourself. God knew that you would face fears in your life, and He has given you loaded promises to claim so you can fight back. What is the truth you need to tell yourself? Write it out so that you can see it.

"The process of overcoming a fear memory is known as 'fear extinction.'"[17] You can create a new response to the fear-inducing stimulus by making new, positive associations with the very thing that scared you.

As a Christian, you can combat your fear and practice fear extinction by using God's truth. Once you have named your fears, you confess them to God. This helps to align your thinking and create new positive neural associations in your brain. Rational thinking involves claiming and applying God's promises to your life. When we claim the promises of God, we are trusting that He will protect us from all of our fears no matter what they are. There is no one more powerful than God; He is omnipotent.

Claim God's promises in your life and use them to fight your fears. For example:

FEAR: I am afraid my boss will fire me soon.
PROMISE: *"The Lord is my light and my salvation—whom shall I fear? The Lord is the stronghold of my life—of whom shall I be afraid?"* (Psalm 27:1).

FEAR: I fear my situation is beyond God's power to help.
PROMISE: *"So do not fear, for I am with you; do not be dismayed,*

17   Op. cit., Vasquez.

for I am your God. I will strengthen you and help you; I will uphold you with my righteous right hand," (Isaiah 41:10).

FEAR: I am afraid that my health will keep getting worse, and I will die a painful death.

PROMISE: *"Do not be anxious about anything, but in everything by prayer and supplication with thanksgiving let your requests be made known to God. And the peace of God, which surpasses all understanding, will guard your hearts and your minds in Christ Jesus,"* (Philippians 4:6–7).

FEAR: I am afraid that God doesn't love me anymore.

PROMISE: *"For I am convinced that neither death nor life, neither angels nor demons, neither the present nor the future, nor any powers, neither height nor anything else in all creation, will be able to separate us from the love of God that is in Christ Jesus our Lord,"* (Romans 8:38–39).

FEAR: I am afraid tomorrow will be even worse than today.

PROMISE: *"Do not worry about tomorrow, for tomorrow will worry about itself,"* (Matthew 6:34).

FEAR: I am afraid of losing my job.

PROMISE: *"And my God will meet all your needs according to the riches of his glory in Christ Jesus,"* (Philippians 4:19).

FEAR: I am not good enough to get into a good relationship.

PROMISE: *"So now there is no condemnation for those who belong to Christ Jesus,"* (Romans 8:1).

FEAR: I will always be alone.

PROMISE: God is faithful; He will always be there for you. *"The faithful love of the Lord never ends! His mercies never cease. Great is His faithfulness; His mercies begin afresh each morning,"* (Lamentations 3:22–23, NLT).

FEAR: There is no way I will get through this.

PROMISE: *"God gives power to the weak and strength to the powerless,"* (Isaiah 40:29).

FEAR: I am going to fail.

PROMISE: *"'For I know the plans I have for you,' declares the Lord, 'plans to prosper you and not to harm you, plans to give you hope and a future,'"* (Jeremiah 29:11).

More promises you can claim to fight against your fears.

I sought the Lord, and he answered me; he delivered me from all my fears. (Psalm 34:4)

For you did not receive a spirit that makes you a slave again to fear, but you received the Spirit of sonship. And by him we cry, "Abba, Father." The Spirit himself testifies with our spirit that we are God's children. Now if we are children, then we are heirs—heirs of God and co-heirs with Christ, if indeed we share in his sufferings in order that we may also share in his glory. (Romans 8:15–17)

The Lord shall give thee rest from thy sorrow, and from thy fear. (Isaiah 14:3, KJV)

We can confidently say, "The Lord is my helper; I will not fear; what can man do to me?" (Hebrews 13:6, ESV)

I sought the Lord, and He heard me, and delivered me from all my fears. (Psalm 34:4, NKJV)

Why are you downcast, O my soul? Why so disturbed within me? Put your hope in God, for I will yet praise him, my Savior and my God. (Psalm 42:5)

We are afflicted in every way, but not crushed; perplexed, but not driven to despair; persecuted, but not forsaken; struck down, but not destroyed. (2 Corinthians 4:8–9, ESV)

The Lord is my shepherd, I shall not want. He makes me lie down in green pastures; He leads me beside quiet waters. He restores my soul; He guides me in the paths of righteousness for His name's sake. Even though I walk through the valley of the shadow of death, I fear no evil, for You are with me; Your rod and Your staff, they comfort me. You prepare a table before me in the presence of my enemies; You have anointed my head with oil; my cup overflows. Surely goodness and loving kindness will follow me all the days of my life, and I will dwell in the house of the Lord forever. (Psalm 23:1–6, NKJV)

Humble yourselves, therefore, under the mighty hand of God so that at the proper time he may exalt you, casting all your anxieties on him, because he cares for you. (1 Peter 5:5–7, ESV)

He will wipe away every tear from their eyes, and death shall be no more, neither shall there be mourning, nor crying, nor pain anymore, for the former things have passed away. (Revelation 21:4)

I can do everything through Christ, who gives me strength. (Philippians 4:13)

Trust in the Lord with all your heart and lean not on your own understanding; in all your ways acknowledge Him, and He will make straight your paths." (Proverbs 3:5–6, ESV)

What fears are you allowing to impact your life? With what promises can you cross out those fears? Write down each fear and then combat it with one of God's promises. You cannot just "get over" a fear; you need to combat irrational fears with rational faith.

FEAR:_____

_____

_____

PROMISE:_____

_____

_____

FEAR:_____

_____

_____

PROMISE:_____

_____

_____

FEAR:_____

_____

_____

PROMISE:_____

_____

_____

Nothing can separate you from the love of God. If you lose your job, you don't have to be afraid. God is there with you and will provide for you. If you fear getting old, give that fear to God and let Him give you comfort. If you fear death, commit your life to Jesus and fear no more. If you are afraid of failing as a parent, walk with God daily and let Him guide you in your decisions. No matter what fear you face, you can overcome it by the power of God found in the Word of God. Apply the promises of God to the problems you fear.

STEP 3: COMMIT TO TRUSTING GOD HOUR BY HOUR AND DAY BY DAY.

The third step is to commit to trusting God, submitting your fears to Him as they arise. Trusting in God is our ultimate remedy for fear. This is much easier said than done. The greater our fears, the more distant God feels. Take one of the previous verses you used to combat a fear and personalize it. This will help you to personalize God's Word and trust God.

You could personalize Proverbs 3:5–6 by writing, "I will trust in the Lord with all of my heart and I won't lean on my own understanding; in all of my ways I will acknowledge Him, and He will make my paths straight."

Personalized, 1 Peter 5:5–7 looks like this, "I will humble myself under the mighty hand of God so that at the proper time he may exalt me, casting all my anxieties on him, because he cares for me."

Personalize two or three of the verses above for yourself in writing.

Spend time praying about the fears you have identified. Pray through each one, asking God to help you overcome it. Your fears might not dissipate instantly, so keep bringing them back to God asking Him to chip away at them until they are gone.

Your ability to fight fear with faith directly correlates with your spiritual walk. This is why it is so important to attend a Spirit-filled, life-giving church, participating actively and serving others. Praise God in prayer and through worship music. Ask the Holy Spirit to strengthen you and guide you. Ask God to drive fear from your life and walk in grace with Him every day. Read the Bible daily, confess your sins and fears, and be authentic with others. You can overcome irrational chronic fears and find peace. This will take you one step closer to the goal of feeling wonderful.

CHAPTER 4

ANGER

The Incredible Hulk has always been a favorite character of mine. The storyline is based on a fictitious man named Dr. Bruce Banner. In an experiment gone wrong, Dr. Banner turns into a giant green muscular Hulk every time he becomes angry. Rage triggers this transformation from man to beast. When Dr. Banner becomes the Hulk, he is bent on destroying the threat, causing enormous carnage in the process. But Dr. Banner hates being the Hulk. For good reason, he doesn't like the beast he turns into when he becomes angry. Once he turned into the Hulk and hurt his beloved girlfriend. Ever since that tragic event, he embarked on a quest to cure himself from turning into the raging monster.

You don't turn into the Hulk when anger gains control of your emotions, but you might display similar characteristics, hurting yourself and others around you. Everyone has a little Hulk in them because anger is a completely normal human emotion. But when anger rages unchecked it leads to many problems at work and home. Lingering and residual anger tends to flare up, making connecting with others difficult. Like Dr. Banner, we may fear the fury of the Hulk within.

By his mid-thirties Todd, was on his way up the corporate ladder. He had energy and a passion for doing things right. His very nature made him the go-to guy in his company when results were needed. But Todd often took on more than he could handle. A major client threw a fit over a minor problem and decided to take her business elsewhere. Todd's boss knew it wasn't his fault but vented on him anyway. An hour later, Todd called it a day, climbed into his car, and drove home. As soon as he turned into the driveway, he had to jam on the brakes, nearly crushing his kids' bikes. He had warned Joey and Samantha about leaving their bikes in the middle of the driveway before—obviously his words were not a strong enough deterrent. After moving the bikes, he pulled into the garage, got out of his vehicle, and stepped into the mudroom, only to find toys scattered everywhere. That is when he came unglued, turning into the Hulk.

For the next ten minutes, Todd yelled, screamed, and threw toys. He blamed his wife for the mess and belittled his kids, destroying their self-esteem and sense of safety. Eventually, his anger subsided and the Hulk turned back into Todd, but it was too late. The kids were crying, his wife silently stared at the ground, and a deep sense of guilt pressed down on Todd. Realizing what he had done, he left the room emotionally torn, returning several minutes later after regaining his composure. Swearing it would never happen again, he apologized to his wife and kids. But this wasn't the first time the Hulk came out, and it wouldn't be the last.

Just down the road, forty-two-year-old Cindy secretly tries to subdue the lurking Hulk within her. Years ago, in college, her longtime boyfriend broke up with her and erroneously told others it was because she was a slut. His slander crushed her, disrupting and impacting her entire life. Instead of dealing with the pain and moving on, she let an angry Hulk move in. She became so obsessed with getting even that the Hulk was always lingering just below the surface, trying to run her life. She found deep satisfaction trashing her ex-boyfriend on social media. Several years later, in her first career job, she got into a verbal argument with her supervisor and was fired. One thing always seemed to lead to another, and the Hulk started to come out more easily and more often as time passed.

Today, Cindy struggles to maintain deep friendships because she knows the Hulk is ever-present but doesn't know how to evict it. She feels hopeless and fearful, choosing to retreat in isolation rather than risk lashing out in a fit of rage. She has prayed, asking God for help, but help always eludes her. She refuses to share her feelings with her closest friend because she is embarrassed. Her inner fight to subdue the Hulk has reached a stalemate.

Todd and Cindy are not two isolated examples of people who struggle with feelings of anger. There are doctors, politicians, teachers, pipe fitters, office managers, and CEOs struggling to control their feelings of anger right now. Chances are you know someone you would identify as having an anger problem and, if you are honest with yourself, you may struggle with anger, too.

According to research:

◉ Almost one-third of Americans say they have a close friend or family member who has trouble controlling their anger.

- More than one in ten (12%) say they have trouble controlling their own anger.
- More than one in four people (28%) say they worry about how angry they sometimes feel.
- One in five of people (20%) say they have ended a relationship or friendship with someone because of how they behaved when they were angry.
- Fewer than one in seven (13%) of those people who say they have trouble controlling their anger have sought help for their anger problems.[18]

Anger, in and of itself, isn't a sin. The Old Testament records that God got angry about 375 times. Jesus was angry with the Pharisees on several occasions and even used a whip to chase people out of the temple courtyard who were spiritually abusing others by overcharging for goods and sacrifices. Jesus demonstrated righteous anger and didn't sin even though He was angry.

While I was in the Air Force, I played hockey for our military base team in Germany. We traveled all over Germany and the Netherlands playing hockey against different European teams, and I had a blast doing it. I am a big guy, and I played defense. Back then, I kind of liked to take my anger out in the rink. If I had a bad day at work, someone on the ice was going to feel it. If someone teased me and I wasn't in a mood to hear it, someone on the ice was going to receive the brunt of my anger by getting checked into the boards. One particular day, our home arena in Bitburg, Germany was packed with fans, including the two-star

---

18   John Shinerrer, "Statistics on the Growing Anger Epidemic," Feb. 21, 2017 (https://webangermanagement.com/statistics-on-the-growing-anger-epidemic), accessed November 1, 2017.

general base commander, who loved hockey. We always drew a large crowd who loved to watch us play. I must have had a bad day at work because ,when I hit the ice, I was ready to rock someone's world. I don't remember what German team we were playing; all I know is there was a guy on the team that I didn't like. He was about six feet tall and had a brown, overgrown beard. We went at it a little in the first period, then a little bit more in the second period. He elbowed me in the corner. I slashed him a few times in the legs. By the time the third period started, I was ready to win one for America.

When the hockey puck went to the corner of the ice rink, I skated toward the puck and so did Ogre. We both checked each other and started slashing at the puck. Unfortunately, I missed the puck and slashed him. So he pushed me back. I threw off my gloves, grabbed his jersey, and rained down a dozen well-earned punches on his face. The Ogre took a wild swing and managed to catch me in the mouth, knocking out my right front tooth. All of this happened in front of a roaring crowd, directly in front of the base commander who witnessed everything. The Ogre and I got ejected from the game, and our team ended up winning without me. It felt good to fight at the time, but my mouth hurt like crazy.

The next day, I went to the dentist to have him put in a fake tooth. He worked on my mouth for what seemed like an eternity before saying he didn't have an exact fit. Instead of ordering the right tooth, he decided to install a tooth from his inventory. After cementing it into my mouth, he ground away on it until he was satisfied. Then he told me to open and close my mouth a few times to see if it fit without rubbing. When he was done, he asked, "Can you chew, boy?" I said I could, but that the tooth didn't feel right. It felt big and tipped outward. The tooth actually felt like I had a Chicklet shoved into my mouth sideways. It made it difficult to talk. When I looked in the mirror, I was instantly aware that the tooth was the wrong color, the wrong size, and was, in fact, tipped outward. But the military isn't about aesthetics, so he said it was good enough and sent me on my way.

That afternoon, I happened to be walking to my office and passed General Stark, the base commander, going out to his car. He recognized me and shouted, "Hey Braland, come here."

So I did. I saluted.

And he said, "Let me see that new smile." I opened my mouth and he shouted "Good God, son!"

I answered, "Well, the dentist said he didn't have the right tooth and asked me if I could chew, and since I said yes he said it was good enough."

General Stark said, "Follow me."

We marched right back into his office, and he called the dentist. After chewing him out, General Stark ordered him to fix my broken tooth correctly. He slammed the phone down and told me to go back to the dentist right away. A mere two hours after my new tooth had been installed, it came right back out again. The dentist took new measurements and ordered the right tooth. At a later date, he installed it perfectly.

Unless we deal with our anger, it will always come out somewhere. My anger used to come out on the hockey rink and with my fists. My Hulk loves to fight. He came out at work and home through my attitude, my lips, my judgmental looks, and my short temper. Regrettably, my anger has spewed onto others in the way I looked at them or talked to them. I have certainly lacked compassion with my words and actions. To this day, my false tooth is a reminder of how I used to deal with my anger in inappropriate ways.

Your anger might come out in foul language, unkind actions, cynicism, or through treating people with disdain. Your anger will always spill over onto your family, kids, spouse, friends, coworkers, and others unless you subdue it. Unchecked anger locked inside will always leak out at some point.

What triggers feelings of anger?

Anger-triggers vary from person to person. Anything and everything can trigger intense feelings of anger that may turn into fits of rage. In my experience, I have worked with people who have such deep feelings of anger they almost seem bi-polar. They laugh and joke and then a memory or circumstance triggers their anger, affecting their entire demeanor. They tense up, look intently at the floor, or start pacing. Living with someone who struggles to control anger creates an unsafe environment for everyone in the home. Since specific anger triggers vary, we will consider only these common ones.

1. HURT.

Anger can come from an emotional hurt or physical hurt. Physical pain can cause short-term anger, but emotional hurt can have lasting effects. For example, one in three divorced people feels intense anger toward their ex even ten years after the divorce. Why? Because divorce hurts.

An emotional hurt caused intense anger in Samson after Samson married a Philistine woman and then her father gave her to another man (see Judges 14–15). Samson burned their fields in anger. In retaliation they burned her and her father to death. So he killed more of them. The cycle of hurt and anger repeated itself over and over until Samson died. All of this anger originated from an emotional hurt.

2. FRUSTRATION.

Frustration, which is similar to anger, is the typical emotional response to opposition, annoyance, or disappointment. It happens when something (real or perceived) interferes with a person's desired goal. Frustrated, unmet expectations often manifest themselves in anger.

Frustration can be both internal and external. Internal frustration can come not only from failing to fulfill one's personal goals or desires but also from coming up against one's perceived deficiencies. Interpersonal conflict can also be a source of internal frustration. External causes of frustration involve conditions outside an individual's control. Examples of such frustrating circumstances could include a long line at a drive-through, a traffic jam, a physical roadblock, a seemingly impossible task, or the perception that time is being wasted.

Some people cope with frustration with passive-aggressive behavior or violence. They may self-medicate with drugs, alcohol, isolating, or media-binges. By far, the most common result of frustration includes anger at some level or another.

Even Jesus' disciples dealt with frustration that turned into anger. On one occasion, they wanted to call down fire from heaven to kill some of the people who opposed them. Their desires were certainly motivated by their frustration toward those who opposed them (see Luke 9:54).

3. INSECURITY.

Uncertainty or anxiety about oneself can result in feelings of insecurity. Insecurity can also come from a lack of self-confidence. Insecurity is a significant contributor to anger. Insecure people who think a coworker is outperforming them may react by gossiping, slandering, or verbally attacking the coworker in hope that the person may get fired or demoted. Insecurity can also stem from being rejected or failing. Often people who feel rejected will feel angry at whomever rejected them, and they may also carry negative thoughts toward themselves. To state it another way: A person who feels like a failure may internalize those feelings and become angry at him- or herself. Feeling insecure makes us more prone to act out in anger in an attempt to get revenge or justice.

The Old Testament describes King Saul as a strong, handsome man who stood tall and looked like a king. The problem was, he was incredibly insecure, and his insecurity caused him to lash out in anger at David. Saul viewed David as a threat because the people loved David. Instead of celebrating David's accomplishments, Saul lashed out in a jealous rage, attempting to kill David several times (see 1 Samuel 18:8).

4. UNMET EXPECTATIONS.

Social activist Elliott Larsen is quoted as saying, "Anger always comes from frustrated expectations." Frustrated expectations are unmet expectations. We anticipate a certain result, and it fails to happen.

Everyone has expectations. For example, when you come home from work you expect the house to be in order, or in the same shape you left it. When you go to the gym, you expect the machines to be clean and in working order. You expect the kids to go to bed on time. You expect your coworkers to turn in their work on time. If you tell your kids to clean the house by the time you get home from work and they don't, you may get angry. If you expect the cable technician to show up at 10:00 a.m. and he shows up at 3:00 p.m., you may get angry. Your needs or desires were not fulfilled as you expected them to be. Such unmet expectations quickly turn into feelings of anger.

Jonah experienced feelings of anger over unmet expectations. God told him to go to Nineveh to warn the people to repent and turn back to God. But Jonah didn't want God to save the Ninevites, so he ran the other way. God used a big fish to bring him to Nineveh. Jonah then did what God wanted him to, and sure enough, the people repented. What was Jonah's response? He was angry at the Lord's compassion toward the Ninevites. So he internalized his anger and pouted.

He prayed to the Lord, "Isn't this what I said, Lord, when I was still at home? That is what I tried to forestall by fleeing to Tarshish. I knew that you are a gracious and compassionate God, slow to anger and abounding in love, a God who relents from sending calamity. Now, Lord, take away my life, for it is better for me to die than to live. (Jonah 4:2–3)

Jonah's unmet expectations with God turned into anger. He didn't want the Ninevites to turn to God; he wanted God to smoke them because the Ninevites were Israel's enemies. But God had other plans. Jonah pouted and complained over God's response. Jonah wanted them all to die, not to repent. His anger came out in his actions and attitude.

Four Expressions of Anger

There are four common expressions of anger. Knowing how you respond when you feel angry helps you begin the journey of healing because you can identify your feelings and become aware of your default response, which enables you to think before you act. Three of the anger expressions are negative; one is positive. The goal is to understand how you express anger so you will be more self-aware, and knowing what triggered those feelings, and plan how you will react to them.

1. AGGRESSIVE.

Those who express anger aggressively can be direct and forceful with others. Their voices become louder, they get stubborn, they tend to be repetitive during arguments, and their outburst is out of proportion to the situation or problem.

Someone who expresses anger aggressively is like a teapot. This person appears calm until the boiling point is reached. At the boiling point, they yell, scream, blame, rant, and rave to let off steam. Everyone around knows when this person vents, someone is going to get burned. After the person cools off, he or she usually feels guilty and ashamed of the outburst.

Moses expressed his anger aggressively. Throughout his life he blew up multiple times. When he was a young man, he blew up on an Egyptian he saw beating the Hebrews, killed him, and buried him in the sand. Later in his life, he became so angry with the Israelites that he struck the rock at Horeb with his staff in anger because the people wouldn't stop whining.

Take the staff, and you and your brother Aaron gather the assembly together. Speak to that rock before their eyes and it will pour out its water. You will bring water out of the rock for the community so they and their livestock can drink. So Moses took the staff from the Lord's presence, just as he commanded him. He and Aaron gathered the assembly together in front of the rock and Moses said to them, "Listen, you rebels, must we bring you water out of this rock?" Then Moses raised his arm and struck the rock twice with his staff. Water gushed out, and the community and their livestock drank. But the Lord said to Moses and Aaron, "Because you did not trust in me enough to honor me as holy in the sight of the Israelites, you will not bring this community into the land I give them." (Numbers 20:8–12)

God told Moses to speak to the rock and water would come out. But Moses was angry, so he took his staff, smacked the rock twice, and yelled at the people. This act of anger bothered God so much that He told Moses he wasn't going to be the one to lead the people into the Promised Land.

2. SUPPRESSIVE.

People who suppress their anger can often come across as having their lives all together. They don't like others to know they have personal problems and are hesitant to share with others. They can be depressed and moody, avoiding conversations about sensitive subjects. Those who suppress their anger won't admit to being angry, yet they live on the edge of exploding all the time.

Think of the person who suppresses anger as a Crock-Pot. Instead of blowing up and letting off steam they sit back, take it all in, letting it cook. Every time their anger is triggered, they stuff their feelings into the pot. Suppressed anger can be felt in the stomach, throat, back, head, or some other place in the body.

Have you ever cooked anything for too long in a Crock-Pot? One morning before my wife, Kathi, left for work, she put some carrots, meat, and potatoes in the Crock-Pot so it would be ready by dinner. But we were delayed and didn't make it home for dinner. Instead of being turned off at 4:00 p.m. when she was supposed to be home, the food continued to cook until 10:00 p.m. Six hours of extra cooking time turned everything into a nasty mush. The combination of heat and time ruined it, rendering it inedible. If you "stuff and stew," you will feel like mush and become as unpleasant as our dinner did.

Jeremiah was a prominent prophet in the Old Testament, and he suppressed his anger, letting it cook in his heart and never really dealing with his feelings in a healthy way. He is known as the "weeping prophet" for good reason.

I never sat in the company of revelers, never made merry with them; I sat alone because your hand was on me and you had filled me with indignation. Why is my pain unending and my wound grievous and incurable? You are to me like a deceptive brook, like a spring that fails. (Jeremiah 15:17–18)

If you perpetually suppress and internalize your anger, it will impact your emotional, spiritual, and physical health in a negative way. You will feel more depressed, angry, withdrawn, frustrated, and tense. You will have problems with other people. You will come across as distant, uninvolved, or uncaring. It's hard to have any significant relationships if you display these characteristics because people will not feel connected to you.

3. PASSIVE-AGGRESSIVE.

One of the best examples of passive-aggressive anger comes from an old novel. Robert Louis Stevenson brought to life Dr. Henry Jekyll and his alternative personality, Mr. Edward Hyde, in the fictional book, *Strange Case of Dr. Jekyll and Mr. Hyde*, published in 1886. As the story goes, Dr. Jekyll feels he is battling between good and bad within himself. He spends his life trying to repress evil urges that are not fitting for a man of high society.

He develops a serum in an attempt to mask this indwelling evil. However, the serum transforms the friendly Dr. Jekyll into Hyde, a hideous creature without compassion or remorse. Hyde is violent and devious. As time passes, Hyde grows in power and shows up anytime Dr. Jekyll shows signs of moral or physical weakness, even without any serum.

Jekyll and Hyde demonstrate passive-aggressive traits to which we all can relate. People who deal with anger in a passive-aggressive manner sulk and pout. They procrastinate when given an undesirable task. They lie, telling others everything is fine, and they blame others for mistakes. Passive-aggressive people can be your best friend one minute and your worst enemy as soon as they leave the room.

Jonah dealt with his anger in a passive-aggressive manner. Jonah was angry that God wanted to save the city of Nineveh. So when God saved the people of Nineveh, that meant Jonah didn't get his way. In response, he became angry, choosing to sit and complain.

But to Jonah this seemed very wrong, and he became angry. He prayed to the Lord, "Isn't this what I said, Lord, when I was still at home? That is what I tried to forestall by fleeing to Tarshish. I knew that you are a gracious and compassionate God, slow to anger and abounding in love, a God who relents from sending calamity. Now, Lord, take away my life, for it is better for me to die than to live."
But the Lord replied, "Is it right for you to be angry?" Jonah had gone out and sat down at a place east of the city. There he made himself a shelter, sat in its shade and waited to see what would happen to the city. Then the Lord God provided a leafy plant and made it grow up over Jonah to give shade for his head to ease his discomfort, and Jonah was very hap-

py about the plant. But at dawn the next day God provided a worm, which chewed the plant so that it withered. When the sun rose, God provided a scorching east wind, and the sun blazed on Jonah's head so that he grew faint.

He wanted to die, and said, "It would be better for me to die than to live." But God said to Jonah, "Is it right for you to be angry about the plant?" "It is," he said. "And I'm so angry I wish I were dead." (Jonah 4:1–9)

I find it delightfully ironic that God provided a shady vine, then sent a worm to destroy it. As if that wasn't bad enough, God turned up the heat and provided a scorching hot wind. Jonah became more and more angry and wanted to die.

4. ASSERTIVE.

Assertive expressions of anger are typically positive expressions of anger. People who express anger assertively can be frustrated without blaming others. They don't make threatening or intimidating remarks and accept responsibility for their mistakes. When anger is expressed directly and in a non-threatening way, it helps people resolve problems without escalating them. A person expressing assertive anger makes statements like, "I feel angry when you gossip about me to coworkers." This statement is direct, assertive, and clear. Other examples of assertive expressions of anger are:

"I am feeling angry because you did not call me when you said you would."

"Your actions were very disrespectful toward me."

"The words you chose to describe my work were very hurtful."

Those who express anger in an assertive manner know they have a responsibility to protect their own rights, feelings, and beliefs. They respect others but not necessarily their behavior. They don't look at every situation as a win-lose event but rather as a win-win opportunity. Learning to express anger in an assertive manner is a skill that can be mastered over time.[19]

Jesus expressed anger assertively. Jesus drove the moneychangers out of the temple courts because they were taking advantage of their own people. In addition, they were preventing the Gentiles from worshipping in the only area of the temple where they were allowed to worship (Matthew 21:12). He also expressed assertive anger when His disciples tried to prevent people from bringing their children to Him (Mark 10:14).

What is your default response to anger?

_____

_____

_____

_____

What is your secondary response to anger?

_____

_____

_____

_____

You Can Change

Unlike the Hulk, you can change. Now that you have a handle on how you deal with anger, the next decision is, what you are going to do about it? All of us have triggers that make us angry, but what we choose to do with them is up to us. You can react to

19   See Christine Hammond, "The Exhausted Woman," PsychCentral, October 12, 2017 (https://pro.psychcentral.com/exhausted-woman/2015/09/healthy-and-unhealthy-expressions-of-anger), accessed November 2, 2018.

the stimulus with godly wisdom or let the Hulk run wild. You don't have to express your anger aggressively, hurting other people as you let off steam. You don't have to internalize your anger and let it turn your heart to mush. You don't need to deal with your anger in a passive-aggressive manner. Instead, you can express anger assertively, strengthening relationships in the process.

Once you understand what triggers your feelings of anger and how you typically respond to those feelings, the next step is to actually deal with the root cause. Generally speaking, anger is a symptom of a greater problem. There is usually something going on inside of us that causes the anger. Anger is the reaction side of an underlying issue.

There was a huge fire a few years ago in California at a large recycling center. Old tires, cardboard boxes, mattresses, electronics and much more were piled in a heap awaiting shredding. Investigators speculate that, while employees were shredding the discarded items, a lithium battery sparked and igniting a roaring fire that burned the plant to the ground, sending toxic smoke into the atmosphere.[20]

In the same way, we shelve so many unresolved issues in our hearts that it doesn't take much to ignite an angry fire. We recycle issues but we never really resolve them. We repeatedly bring up the past, get angry at people who have died or moved out of our lives long ago, and fantasize about getting even or beating them at their own sick game. The more unresolved issues we accumulate, the bigger the risk of an anger explosion triggered by a single

20   Jeffrey A. Fowler, "The explosive problem with recycling iPads, iPhones and other gadgets: They literally catch fire," *The Washington Post*, September 11, 2018 (https://www.washingtonpost.com/technology/2018/09/11/explosive-problem-with-recycling-ipads-iphones-other-gadgets-they-literally-catch-fire/?noredirect=on&utm_term=.c68d93171eab), accessed November 7, 2018.

spark. All it takes is an ignition source to start a raging fire. Often the explosion happens at the point of least resistance. People who are not even part of the initial problem can become sucked into the crossfire and may even become wounded themselves. We end up hurting our precious children, spouse, employees, and friends. People get hurt when anger piles up. The Apostle Paul wrote,

Let all bitterness and wrath and anger and clamor and slander be put away from you, along with all malice. And be kind to one another, tender-hearted, forgiving each other, just as God in Christ also has forgiven you. (Ephesians 4:31–32)

One of the cool things about our humanity is our ability to adjust our default response to anger. You have the God-given ability to interject rational thinking between the stimulus and the response. Nobody can "make you mad." You choose how you respond to feelings of anger. Have you ever argued with your spouse or yelled at your kids on your way to church or somewhere else? You might argue like crazy but once you arrive at the destination and get out of the car you quickly greet others with a smile. You are not preprogrammed to lose control of your emotions. You can choose to defuse your anger.

This is where the rubber meets the road. Here are three steps to help you manage your anger and move from wounded to wonderful.

1. ADMIT YOU ARE ANGRY.

Men in particular really struggle to be in touch with their emotions, often denying feelings of anger. We spend so much time trying to mask our emotions that we have a tough time admitting when we feel angry. So the first step when you get angry is to admit you are angry, to yourself and to God. The apostle Paul wrote, *"Be angry, and yet do not sin; do not let the sun go down on your anger, and do not give the devil opportunity,"* (Ephesians 4:26–27). Paul says when anger is present, you should acknowledge it and then control it. God does not want you to hang on to unresolved anger. If you do, you will compromise your faith, opening an opportunity for the devil to use it for evil.

2. IDENTIFY THE REAL SOURCE OF YOUR ANGER.

In my past, I have come home from work and yelled at the kids for trashing the house before gathering all the facts surrounding why the house was trashed. Maybe Kathi had an emergency to deal with. I don't know, and until I gather more information, I might make a poor judgment and express my anger aggressively. I have been short with Kathi for forgetting to pay a bill. The truth is, I have forgotten to pay bills, but for some reason, I do not lash out at myself. If I am honest with myself, sometimes when I am angry with my family it actually has nothing to do with them. I am really angry with someone or something that happened someplace else. It's called "displaced anger," and I expressed displaced anger often.

When you identify the real source of your anger, you need to ask God to shine His searchlight on your heart. What things in your life need to be revealed? Is it pride, selfishness, ungodly goals, or a responsibility that you must pay attention to? James wrote, *"What causes fights and quarrels among you? Don't they come from your desires that battle within you?"* (James 4:1).

Maybe the real source of your anger is rooted in an unmet expectation, frustration, hurt, or low self-esteem. Can you put your finger on what your source of anger is? Identifying the true source of your anger is essential. If you don't, you will never get to the root cause of the emotion.

3. IDENTIFY WHERE YOU FEEL THE ANGER IN YOUR BODY.

Do you feel it in your stomach? In your legs? Your back? It is lingering in your flesh and bones somewhere. Identify where you feel it so you can start to control it. You are not the Hulk. You can control it because you are a child of God. When I get angry, I feel it in my stomach. I start to lose my voice, and my throat burns. The cause of the pain is a medical problem related to acid reflux, but it is exacerbated by how I have learned to cope with my anger. I have conditioned myself to stuff anger instead of neutralizing it.

4. SPEAK OUT HOW YOU FEEL WHEN YOU ARE ANGRY.

Do you want to "rip their head off" (metaphorically speaking)? Do you want to scream? Do you want to cry? Hit something or someone?

Get in touch with your emotions and your feelings when you are angry. Stop suppressing your feelings and acknowledge them. Search for them in your past if you have to. There is power in transparency. Use your mouth to speak out loud how you feel. Find a safe place to yell into a pillow, or shout it out in your car with the windows up.

5. SURRENDER YOUR ANGER AND ALL OF ITS ATTENDING EMOTIONS TO GOD.

The only way to diffuse raw anger is to surrender it to the real, living God. As James 4:11–12 states, God is the judge, not you or me. So often we want to get revenge for whatever it is that caused us to get angry. We want to cut off the other driver, yell at that jerk of a client, or punch that gossip in the face. In other words, we want to judge and punish the offender. But God is the real judge, not you or me. *"Do not take revenge, my dear friends, but leave room for God's wrath, for it is written: 'It is mine to avenge; I will repay,' says the Lord,"* (Romans 12:19).

6. LET THE HOLY SPIRIT MOVE YOU TO RIGHT-EOUS ACTION OR BRING YOU TO BROKENNESS.

You might need to take righteous action and talk to the person who wounded you. If you do, do it in such a way that brings glory to God. In other words, don't just go yell at them, punch them, or break their stuff. Let the Holy Spirit lead the reconciliation process and enter into it with no expectation that the person will own up to their actions. You can only "own" your part and your feelings. You are not responsible for their response. Christians are not doormats. You don't have to tolerate injustice or offenses without taking action. You can speak the truth in love.

On the other hand, you might need to let the Holy Spirit bring you to a place of brokenness. Brokenness involves repenting from sin, accepting the past hurt as a past hurt, and asking God to give you peace by surrendering the situation or person to God, trusting His righteous judgment. This is hard. The point isn't to let the other person get away with it, it's to relieve you of carrying the pain anymore. Give it to God. This takes faith and trust.

When firemen fight fires, they often shoot water into the pile of rubble long after the flames are gone. Why is this? The reason the firefighters keep shooting water into the pile of rubble is because there are often hot spots smoldering deep in the rubble that can ignite again.

Your heart can have hot spots too. Spots that flare up from time to time when you least expect it because you haven't dealt with the anger stuck in your heart. Sure, you are quick to extinguish the flames on the outside and mask some of your feelings, but unless you take care of the source of the anger, you will have flare-ups. You need the Holy Spirit to get to the center of the ignition source.

Talking about dealing with anger is one thing, actually taking the steps to move from wounded to wonderful is another. I want to help you to move from wounded to wonderful by dealing with root causes of anger. The apostle Paul wrote, *"Bear with each other and forgive one another if any of you has a grievance against someone. Forgive as the Lord forgave you,"* (Colossians 3:13).

If you are ready to take a step of faith and deal with your anger, here is what to do.

1. On a blank piece of paper, write down any feelings of anger you have. Describe your feelings in detail. Why are you angry? Who offended you? What unmet expectation is present in your feelings? Are you angry with yourself?

2. Write down where you feel the anger in your body.

3. Does your anger have a color? If so, what color is it? Write it down.

4. What words did you say out loud? What words do you still need to say?

The anger you have been carrying around in your heart is

now on the paper. The next step is to surrender it to God. Take the piece of paper you have written on and tear it in half. Now tear it in half again. Walk to the nearest trash can and take the torn paper that represents your anger and toss it in the trash can. Repeat these words out loud, "I release my anger, tearing it out of my life once and for all. By removing my anger, I am making room for more of God in my life. Holy Spirit, I ask that You fill the void with Your love and grace. Amen."

This outward act is symbolic of giving God what is in your heart. You will feel free after you do it. Do not skip this step! Speak audibly; there is power in your words.

Write down the date you did this, the time you did this, and the place where you did this. Be specific. It will make the experience real.

After you trash your anger, you will have room in your heart for peace. If you have been mad at yourself, ask God to forgive you for whatever you did, and step into freedom. If you need to forgive someone, do the best you can to start that process today. The psalmist wrote, *"The Lord gives strength to his people; the Lord blesses his people with peace,"* (Psalm 29:11).

Write this verse out on a blank piece of paper. Once you write it down, put it in a prominent place where you will see it often. It will remind you that God blesses His people with peace, the peace that you need in your life.

Congratulations on actually leaning into the anger that has been in your heart. Now you have the tools to eradicate your anger and not just recycle it. There will be times when you feel angry over past issues again, so don't get discouraged. Deal with those feelings every time they surface and eventually they will surface less and less often. This will give you more confidence because you won't fear transforming into the Hulk at just the wrong time. With God's help and a humble heart, you can work through your anger and learn to express yourself in a godly way.

CHAPTER 5

FROM SHAME *to* REDEMPTION

An older man lived alone in the country. It was spring, and he wanted to dig his tomato garden, as he had done every year. He loved his tomatoes and liked to can them and make tomato sauce and salsa. But tilling the garden by hand was very hard for the old man now. He had always relied on his son to till the garden so he could do the planting. Unfortunately, his only son had gotten into some legal trouble and was in prison. The old man wrote a letter to his son and described his predicament:

> *Dear son,*
> *I am feeling pretty bad because it looks like I won't be able to plant my tomato garden this year. I'm just getting too old to be tilling the garden. The soil is hard and heavy. If only you were here, my troubles would be over. I know you would till the garden for me.*
> *Love, Dad*

A few days later, he received a letter from his son:

Dear Dad,

Do not dig up the garden! That is exactly where I buried the bodies.

Love, Your son.

At 4:00 the next morning, FBI agents and local police arrived at the old man's house and dug up the entire garden from corner to corner. However, they didn't find any bodies, so they apologized to the old man and left. Later that same day, the old man received another letter from his son.

Dear Dad,

Go ahead and plant the tomatoes now. That's the best I could do for you under the circumstances.

Love, Your son.

Although that fictitious story is hilarious, it illustrates a powerful and painful reality. Everyone has a little shame buried someplace in their past. Shame is the intensely painful feeling or experience of believing we are flawed and therefore unworthy of love and belonging. Shame makes you feel like you have nothing to give or nothing to contribute and are therefore unworthy of connection.

Shame is a painful emotion responding to a sense of failure to attain some ideal state. Shame encompasses the entire self. The thought process in shame involves self-focused attention. The physical expressions of shame include the blushing face, slumped with head down, eyes averted. It generates a wish to hide, to disappear or even to die.[21]

---

21 Dr. Shahram Heshmat, "5 Factors That Make You Feel Shame...and how to get rid of it," *Psychology Today*, October 4, 2015 (https://www.psychologytoday.com/us/blog/science-choice/201510/5-factors-make-you-feel-shame), accessed June 28, 2018.

When shame is internalized, it is incredibly harmful. The story line changes from what was done to who we are. Psychologists refer to "toxic shame" as the feeling that one is fundamentally and wholly inadequate of love.[22]

Shame and guilt often go together, but they are not the same.

Guilt

Guilt is feeling bad for something you screwed up. You feel guilty when you lose your temper or spend too much money. Guilt is usually short-lived and temporary. Guilt involves a negative evaluation of a specific behavior. It is typically a less painful experience than shame because the object of disapproval is a specific behavior, not the entire self.[23]

Guilt is an emotion that can motivate a person to take corrective action, as in apologizing for making crass comments or acting inappropriately at a party.

Shame is a deeper longer-lasting feeling.

Shame

Shame is caused by an awareness of guilt or some disgraceful action. Shame is the emotion that convinces you that you are a lousy mother because you can't bake like Rachael Ray, your laundry isn't done up to Tide standards, and you missed your fourth grader's field trip last year. You thumb through social media, fixated on all the other rock-star moms with amazing kids, bubbly smiles, and gorgeous homes, feeling worse and worse about yourself as you scroll down. Everyday, you force yourself to

22   Jeremy Deaton, "How shame can take a toll on your emotional health," Headspace.com (https://www.headspace.com/blog/2017/11/02/shame-emotional-health), accessed July 23, 2018.

23   Op. cit., Heshmat.

sit at your work station, your mind filled with self-accusations. Shame points its finger at you, demanding you isolate yourself and live alone. Shame greets you Monday morning in the mirror with "I'm an idiot," "I'm a loser," "I'm a failure," and then sends you to bed with a similar sayonara. Shame makes you label yourself as fat, dumb, Chubby Cheeks, Big Butt, or Lard-O because you haven't lost those frustratingly sticky twenty pounds. Shame keeps you from going to the gym or playing at the pool with the kids. Shame screams, "You fool!" for speaking up at last week's staff meeting, telling everyone how you really feel. Now you're dreading any interaction whatsoever with your boss.

Shame is a powerful emotion that everyone experiences at some time or another. Shame is one of the most negative and debilitating feelings a person can experience because it combines other negative emotions to steamroll a person into a dark pit. People feel ashamed of their negative emotions such as anger, fear, sadness, and lingering guilt. This reinforces a corrosive, negative cycle that is hard to break. We think the little voice in our head is right, the voice that calmly cries out, "I knew you'd fail," "You'll never really belong," and "Who would love you?" We cover our shame with masks, relationships, lies, self-harm, and whatever else works at the time. But the truth is, shame sucks all of the happiness and joy right out of our lives, leaving us relationally and spiritually dehydrated.

Shame both shuts you down and leaks out in destructive ways. It is the gift that keeps on giving because it wounds you over and over and over unless you have the courage to see it for what it is, hand it over to God, and let the love of Christ heal it.

I have stared in the mirror shaming myself for being a poor

husband, father, pastor, friend, and neighbor. Shame has kept me in front of the TV when I could have been out playing with my kids, spending time with friends, or exercising. I have felt intense shame after failing to reach a personal goal or refusing to speak the truth to another person when the truth needed to be spoken.

When my son was nine, I took him to the store to buy plastic BBs for his airsoft gun. The bullets came in a clear plastic container about the size of a soda can. He was thrilled to have the ammo he needed to pelt his targets. After I paid for the BBs, Josh insisted that he carry his proud purchase out of the store. We had almost reached the car when the lid of the container popped off, and the BBs dumped all over the ground. He shouted, "Oh no!" and looked at me. Instead of looking back at him with sympathy and offering to help, I glared at him in frustration. I was angry he hadn't taken greater care in handling the BBs, and now half of the BBs were gone. My reaction was poor. I should have empathized with him and reassured him we could go back into the store and buy more if we needed to. My poor parenting moment caused incredible shame in me for years.

The Effect of Shame on the Body

Shame has been linked to addiction, violence, aggression, depression, eating disorders, and bullying, so it's crucial that you learn ways to deal with it and build healthy barriers against it. Holding onto the emotion of shame can damage your physical health as well. Physiologically your body responds to the emotion of shame causing symptoms such as:

- Nausea
- Chest tightness
- Lethargy

- Flushing skin
- Diverting eye contact
- Digestive problems
- Inflammation
- Lowered immune system

Biblical Examples of People Who Felt Shame

The woman with brown hair and brown sunken eyes woke up to face another difficult day. She had lived a tough life in an unforgiving town. A few bad decisions here and there had led to a nasty reputation. She knew that she had to make another trip to the well, which would take her from the relative safety of her home into the center of the cruel world. So she waited until noon, when few, if any, of the townswomen would be there.

By the time she got to the well, the sun was at its highest and hottest. But what was this? A Jewish man was sitting there, looking right at her.

"Could you please draw some water for me? I am thirsty."

This caught her off guard; Jewish men did not talk to Samaritan women, ever.

She responded, "Yes, but how can you even think of asking for a drink?"

The man said, *"If you only knew who you were talking to you could have living water instead of settling for stale cistern water"* (John 4:10).

Cistern water came from storm runoff or seeped into deep holes from the surrounding ground. It was stale and old. It was drinkable but not very good. Living water was better water. It was fresh water that came from running streams or natural springs.

Living water was the best kind of water because it was pure and delicious. The woman knew what living water was, and she was honestly baffled by His statement.

"Sir," the woman said, "you have nothing to draw with and the well is deep. Where can you get this living water? Are you greater than our father Jacob, who gave us the well and drank from it himself, as did also his sons and his livestock?" (John 4:11–12).

This was so confusing. Maybe there was a religious side to the man's statements. The woman pursued that idea.

The woman said, "I know that Messiah" (called Christ) "is coming. When he comes, he will explain everything to us." Then Jesus declared, "I, the one speaking to you—I am he," (John 4:25–26).

Jesus knew this woman wanted acceptance, forgiveness, and real love. He knew she hated herself. He knew she was hurting. Jesus knew her wounds came from broken relationships. So He addressed it with her, revealing He knew all about her string of ex-husbands. He spoke truth to her and she believed Him.

She went back into her village, freed from shame and with a new story to tell.

Many of the Samaritans from that town believed in him because of the woman's testimony, "He told me everything I ever did." So when the Samaritans came to him, they urged him to stay with them, and he stayed two days. And because of his words many more became believers. They said to the woman, "We no longer believe just because of what you said; now we have heard for ourselves, and we know that this man really is the Savior of the world." (John 4:39–42)

Does this woman's story resonate with you? Do certain places and people remind you of your painful past? The Bible is stuffed with real stories of people who struggled with shame.

The story of the prodigal son described in Luke 15:11–32 is another story related to shame. A young man demanded that his father give him his inheritance before his father died. His dad did, and the son went out and spent it all. There is no doubt that he felt the full weight of shame. He didn't return home when he ran into trouble because he was ashamed of his actions.

It's hard to admit when you have screwed up. We don't want to swallow our pride. We would rather suffer than surface. Eventually, this young man did return home to his father, who poured out his love on him. The story is a great analogy of the way God the Father forgives us for our mistakes instead of shaming us for them.

Luke 18 records a conversation Jesus had with a group of people who thought they had it all together. They thought they lived on the right street, had the best donkey, ate the best food, and had the best kids. These people didn't miss a party and a chance to tell others how awesome they were. They were the ones who started the "humble brag." They looked down on everybody else. But Jesus knew their issues. Jesus saw right past their fancy clothes and fake smiles and spoke directly to their hearts. So He told them a powerful parable to make a significant spiritual point.

To some who were confident of their own righteousness and looked down on everyone else, Jesus told this parable: "Two men went up to the temple to pray, one a Pharisee and the other a tax collector. The Pharisee stood by himself and prayed: 'God, I thank you that I am not like other people—robbers, evildoers, adulterers—or even like this tax collector. I fast twice a week and give a tenth of all I get." (Luke 18:9–12)

The Pharisees were the social elites. They wore white robes, distinguishing themselves from the average person. They wore a head covering to signify that they were set apart. The people actually looked up to them because they were the religious leaders. In the parable, Jesus is pointing out the Pharisee's hypocrisy. He prayed out loud to proclaim how great he was and in doing so denied his own brokenness. His prayer tells us that he thought of himself as much better than everybody else. The text further explains, *"But the tax collector stood at a distance. He would not even look up to heaven, but beat his breast and said, "God, have mercy on me, a sinner,"* (Luke 18:13).

Jesus used tax collectors as examples several times because everyone knew tax collectors were corrupt. Basically, the Romans hired people to collect taxes and said the collectors could keep anything they collected over what the Roman government required. So if the Romans demanded $20 from everyone that week and the tax collector could collect $25 from each person, he stood to make a decent profit for his services. Not all tax collectors collected the same amount; some reaped huge profits and others moderate ones. As long as the Romans were paid the amount they had dictated, it didn't matter how much tax collectors stuffed in their pockets from overcharging.

Tax collectors were running a scam, and everybody knew it. But because people were so afraid of the Roman authorities, they went ahead and paid the required taxes, grumbling about the additional fees. Yet, in the parable, the corrupt tax collector is the one who humbled himself before God, choosing to stand far away from the temple while confessing his shame to God. He was so broken that he didn't even want to look toward heaven, choosing instead a posture of humility. The Pharisee in the parable kept trying to look good in front of God and others, pretending everything was good, while the tax collector humbled himself and confessed what he was ashamed of. Jesus explained, *"I tell you that this man, rather than the other, went home justified before God. For all those who exalt themselves will be humbled, and those who humble themselves will be exalted,"* (Luke 18:14).

This is a beautiful picture of someone who humbled himself before God and asked Him to redeem him from shame. The tax collector had ripped people off, and it was haunting him. He was so full of shame that he couldn't even look to heaven or make eye contact with other people.

I don't want to walk around with shame. I don't want to live my life staring in the rearview mirror. I know you don't either. The good news is that we can find redemption from shame. We can start looking forward to tomorrow instead of mourning the past.

Three Strategies to Eliminate Shame

There are three strategies that will help you step away from the woundedness of shame and move a little closer to wonderful.

1. Cry out to God from a place of brokenness.

Like the tax collector in the parable, we need to humble ourselves before God so He can heal our shame and restore our lives. The Scriptures are full of stories of people who blew it and then cried out to God from a place of brokenness. The psalmist wrote, *"The Lord is close to the brokenhearted and saves those who are crushed in spirit,"* (Psalm 34:18).

This is what the Pharisees just could not seem to do. They could not seem to humble themselves before the Holy God. They never dealt with any of their own problems and hypocrisy. And because they were too proud to be humble, Jesus had a problem with them.

You need to be transparent with your brokenness. Psychologists say that confession is one of the best remedies for breaking free from shame. Cry out to God from a place of brokenness for the purposes of being healed and restored. Take off the fake and get real with God. The ground is level at the foot of the Cross, and Jesus exalts those who humble themselves before God. Healing from shame starts with humility.

This exercise will help you identify the shame you have in your life right now. Answer the following questions:

1. DESCRIBE, in writing, a specific incident from childhood or adolescence in which you felt shame. Articulate the feelings you had during the incident. What thoughts went through your head? What thoughts are still there? How did you feel after the incident?

2. WRITE DOWN where you feel the shame in your body. Do you feel it in your back, head, or stomach? Be specific.

3. IF YOUR SHAME has a color, what color would it be?

4. WHAT sound does shame make? Can you articulate that sound?

5. WHAT texture does your shame have?

6. WRITE DOWN how you think that feeling of shame still influences you today. Does it impact a specific person or group of people? Describe shame's influence in detail.[24]

2. Bring shame into the light.

This involves confessing your feelings with absolute transparency to God. The last thing anyone wants to do is talk about why they feel shame. We worry that if someone finds out how horrible we are, they will run from us, so we learn to cover it and carry on. But when we cover it, we don't actually deal with it. It clings to us, and we always know it's there. The truth is, the more we talk about what shames us, the less power it has over our lives.

Several years ago, I went to my class reunion. It was at a large hotel in one of the spacious meeting rooms big enough to accommodate our high school class of 768 graduates. At one point, I walked past a woman standing with a group of people who knew me. She said "Hi, John! We were just talking about you." I don't know how you might have reacted, but words like those from an old schoolmate scared me. Out of courtesy, I stopped to talk. She continued, "We were just reminiscing about elementary school, and I just shared my most embarrassing moment. It was when you pulled my pants down in front of the whole class in third grade." For a moment, time stood still. I had no recollection of doing such a thing, but she did. She knew when it happened, where it happened, and who did it to her. I felt so ashamed and

---

24   Adapted from "What We Get Wrong About Shame," by Jane Bolton, *Psychology Today*, May 18, 2009 (https://www.psychologytoday.com/us/blog/your-zesty-self/200905/what-we-get-wrong-about-shame), accessed June 28, 2018.

apologized profusely for what I did. She laughed and said, "I'm over it now." I have to wonder how much counseling she had to get because of me. I slipped right back to my table and spent the rest of the night feeling intense shame. It was awful. I could hear that voice in my ear whispering that my past was loaded with far worse stories; that I was a fake because of what I had done. And to be honest, those feelings lasted for several days because I kept telling myself how bad I was.

Then I shared my story with God and let the light of Christ shine on it—that changed how I felt. I didn't have to try to hide my shame; I just let God see all of it. It was so freeing.

It can be very helpful to expose your shame to a trusted friend. Let them know how you feel and why you feel that way. Just airing out your feelings with an empathetic believer is encouraging. Brené Brown gave an inspiring TED talk titled "Listening to Shame," in which she said, "The antidote to feeling shame is a willingness to be vulnerable. To be human is to be imperfect—to have scars and stretch marks, and to cry when sad or afraid." She continued, "If you put shame in a Petri dish, it needs three things to grow exponentially: secrecy, silence, and judgment. If you put the same amount in a Petri dish and douse it with empathy, it can't survive. The two most powerful words when we're in a struggle are: me too."[25]

> *Then I shared my story with God and let the light of Christ shine on it—that changed how I felt. I didn't have to try to hide my shame; I just let God see all of it. It was so freeing.*

Just thinking about your shame can make you want to run and hide, and that's what the enemy wants you to do. However,

---

25   Brené Brown, "Listening to Shame," TEDxHouston2012, (https://www.ted.com/talks/brene_brown_listening_to_shame), accessed July 23, 2018.

God wants you to admit your brokenness and bring it to the light. Share your shame with God. He knows about it anyway. Bringing your shame out of the dark allows it to be diffused by the love of Christ. Let the light of Christ begin to soak into the shadows of your life and bring healing.

Take the piece of paper you wrote on and released your shame by crunching it in your hand. Hold it tightly with a closed fist and pray out loud the following.

"Jesus, right now I give you all of my shame. I put it at the foot of the cross and claim freedom from it. I claim my rights as a child of God—there is no condemnation for me. I will not condemn myself any more. I refuse to let others condemn me. I receive your grace and forgiveness and will walk in it from now on."

Take the crumpled piece of paper and throw it away. You may even want to shred it into a dozen pieces because shame is history and has been dealt with.

3. Claim God's complete healing and redemption.

Now that you have dealt with your shame, start embracing God's truth. The people of the Corinthian church had their share of problems. Many of them had big problems that spilled into every area of their life. Paul didn't rebuke them for their past; he encouraged them about being new creations in Christ. They needed to know the old life with all its shame was gone and the new life with all the joy had come. Paul wrote, *"Therefore, if anyone is in Christ, the new creation has come: The old has gone, the new is here!"* (2 Corinthians 5:17).

A few days after my class reunion, I had to deal with the shame I was feeling because letting my past echo around in my head made it start to grow. I reflected on all that I have failed at, all that I have done wrong, everything for which I wish I could hit the do-over button. Meeting my classmate started a negative spiral in my life that wounded me yet again.

Shame always spanks us where we are most vulnerable. After my friend reminded me of my past, I had to remind myself that I am no longer the person I used to be. I am a new creation in Christ. I was a sinner, but now I have been saved by grace.

There is a good reason Satan wants you to feel shameful. Feeling shameful keeps you from confidently approaching God's throne and having a close personal relationship with Him. The Bible repeatedly clarifies that Jesus died on the cross for *all* of your sins, not just the little ones. He loves you with all your baggage, bumps, and bruises. He loves you in spite of what you have thought, done, and left undone. He loves you and wants to walk with you right now. He wants you to find hope, healing, and your future in His will. That is the power of the cross. That is the power of God manifest in your life, breaking through the shame, instilling freedom and grace. The author of Hebrews wrote, *"Let us draw near with a true heart in full assurance of faith, having our hearts sprinkled from an evil conscience, and our bodies washed with pure water,"* (Hebrews 10:22).

My past doesn't determine my future, and your past doesn't determine your future. You are not who you *were*. Shame ties you to an event you desperately want to cover. But the reality is, the more you cover it, the less you will heal. Leave your shame at the cross and receive the freedom Jesus has for you. Paul wrote, *"Therefore, there is now no condemnation for those who are in Christ Jesus, because through Christ Jesus the law of the Spirit who gives life has set you free from the law of sin and death,"* (Romans 8:1–2).

Matthew Brady is considered by many to be the father of photojournalism. He assembled a team of photographers to document the Civil War. He and his associates traveled throughout the eastern part of the country and photographed many of the battlefields, towns, and people touched by the war. He photographed prominent people like Ulysses S. Grant, George Custer, Stonewall Jackson, and Robert E. Lee. He also captured gruesome scenes of mangled, dead bodies; horrifically wounded soldiers; destroyed towns; burned homes; and war-torn, sad faces. Viewing the pictures triggered painful emotions and profound sadness. Over the course of the war the photographers took over 12,000 pictures and put them on traveling displays. But over time, people became sick of seeing all the horrors of war. They stopped coming to his studios and buying his prints.

In those days, pictures were developed on a glass plate negative which was used to make the prints. Since people were not buying his prints, the glass negatives were not needed. At war's end, deeply in debt, Brady was forced to sell most of the glass plate negatives to starving farmers for pennies. They didn't buy the glass plate negatives for the pictures; they bought them for the glass. They recycled the glass negatives, using them to build greenhouses to grow food that provided sustenance in the midst of the deprivations in the post-war South. When the glass plates were first installed, the pictures of death and destruction could be seen clearly reflected on the plants and floors of the greenhouses. But as the years went by, the sun's rays burned the imagery from the glass, and they became transparent.

Let Christ into the situations you feel ashamed of. Christ can bring healing and hope if you let Him. Expose your shame to Christ then let His light shine through you. Claim God's promise to remove the shame from your life. The psalmist wrote, *"You light a lamp for me. The Lord, my God, lights up my darkness,"* (Psalm 18:28, NLT).

CHAPTER 6

FROM LOSS *to* LIFE

The journey to deal with my wounds had begun at Gate 23D, and now my destination was a beautiful ranch nestled in the middle of spacious Wyoming. After a long, fifteen-hour drive, I pulled into the ranch late at night. Here I would have no access to the internet, limited phone service, no social media, no TV, no interruptions, and no distractions. This was the place of solitude I needed to deal with some of the most painful wounds in my life. It was late fall, and all the vibrant green colors of summer were gone. Now the fields were brown and silent, the pastures empty. As I got out of my truck, I noticed the silence. No road noise; no planes; no loud, nosy neighbors; no radio—just darkness and silence. I thought I would fall asleep quickly in such a serene setting, but I'm used to noise, so I lay restless for the better part of an hour before drifting off.

I was greeted by silence when I awoke, and it sounded great. I read my Bible, ate some food, and then sat at the small dining table staring out the window toward the distant mountains. Instead of diving into some scheduled project as I would normally do, I allowed my mind to drift into the past.

Most of the time, I get distracted or distract myself rather than letting my mind wander too far. Not this day. On this day, I had nowhere to be or anything pressing to do. With my iPad playing soft worship music in the background, my head started to flood with memories.

I recalled with great joy walking with my three young children down the ranch's long, dusty, dirt driveway. I imagined fishing one more time in the mountain irrigation runoff canals for carp, just as we used to do on a daily basis during our vacations here. I stared at the pool, envisioning my family laughing and playing Marco Polo. These were all good memories, and I found myself longing for just one more family trip, one more long walk together, and one more innocent family game of blackjack. The reality I had to face was that those days gone. My kids are all teenagers now. They have school, sports, jobs, and their own relationships to enjoy.

New memories would be made, and they would look different. I knew this in my heart, but something inside of me was stuck. I was tangled in the past, and it was keeping me from enjoying the present and feeling hopeful about the future.

As I stared at the mountains in the distance, my mind drifted deep into the past. I started to feel the pain from all the losses I have experienced over the years. I grieved the death of my childhood best friend, Betsy, when we were five. Now as an adult, I was able to feel a small portion of the pain her parents must have suffered. I recalled with tears the wounded bird I took in when I was nine or ten; I cared for it until it died a week later. At that age, I was crushed, not knowing how to deal with death and loss. When I was thirteen, my grandfather died. He suffered painful brain cancer for a year, and he lost his mind a little bit more every day. I didn't understand why he suffered so much and saw how hard it was on my parents. Then, my mind flooded with fragments of loss in random order. Each memory fragment had pain associated with it in some way, shape, or form.

Shortly after becoming a pastor, I had a great talk with a good friend who was battling depression. He told me how great he was feeling and how much progress he was making. His fiancée, Stacy, stood by his side smiling from ear to ear, soaking in his optimism. Ten hours later, he committed suicide in his garage. Stacy called me right after she called the police, and I immediately dropped everything to drive to their house. With absolute clarity, I recalled that specific moment in time when I met Stacy in her living room and witnessed the ramifications of his irreversible decision. My heart still breaks for his fiancée and their daughter.

Less than a year, later a friend introduced me to Chad and we became friends. He started coming to church and gave his life to Christ. He had a great sense of humor and loved to make others laugh. But he also battled depression. After a series of bad decisions, he didn't want to have anything to do with any of his friends, including me. A couple months later I got the call that he had also taken his own life. I felt crushed, angry, frustrated, and confused all at the same time. I had to drive to his home tell his ex-wife and children that he had taken his own life. I still miss him. I wish these were the only two people I knew who wounded me and so many others by taking their own lives, but they are not.

I began to grieve good relationships that went bad. I have had friends turn on me, badmouth me, blame me, and hurt me. A number of people have left the church I serve at and have broken off their relationship with me. Some left for valid reasons, such as a different youth group or specialty ministries; others left because they felt I knew them too well. One couple clearly felt uncomfortable talking to me in public after she had shared in private during counseling that her husband beats her. One family got angry with a decision that was made and cut me, my wife, and our children out of their lives. Now, when I see them at Target, they walk right past me as if I am a complete stranger. It hurts, and I mourn over the loss of that relationship even though it ended so painfully. Several people have been vocally critical of me on social media. One person wrote a nasty blog about me and made sure to unfriend me only after he knew I read it. Others have severed their relationship with me for untold reasons. It's hard to downplay the pain and loss from broken relationships because the pain is real and the loss evident. Their words cut deep and I felt it. I grieve the loss of such relationships more than anything else.

Several of my best friends have moved out of state in the past few years, and I miss them. Their absence in my life is a form of loss. We still talk on the phone, but it's not the same. The relational loss is real and tangible, and it has impacted my desire to make new friends. The older I get, the more difficult it is to cultivate significant relationships. Relational departures always leave me feeling fragmented, disappointed, and wounded.

After grieving the loss of broken relationships and loss of life, my mind began to grieve the death of many hopes and dreams that will never come to be. I always dreamed that my family would be able to take a great vacation together. I envisioned us driving in the car, laughing and talking with eager anticipation of being together for a week of rest and recreation. But I was so busy at church that I never made time to take the family on any vacations until a few years ago. I grieved the fact that my priorities were screwed up and that I will never be able to regain that lost time.

When our family finally did start to take some vacations, I held firm to my dream of laughing and enjoying one another. Unfortunately, several of our vacations turned out to be a veritable living hell. The kids constantly grumbled, argued, and pestered each other. I became resentful of them, and my relationship with Kathi grew tense because we both wanted to get away from our getaway. To make matters worse, we often went into debt to pay for them. So for several months after a bad vacation, we had to keep paying it off. It felt like paying off a fine. I grieved the death of my dream to build positive memories with my family. Not all of our vacations were bad. Some were good, but on this day I grieved the ones that were not.

I have launched several businesses that failed. I have bought investment properties, expecting to turn a profit, only to lose thousands of dollars to unload them. I have failed in many areas more than once. My past is decorated with dead dreams framed in moments of time, and they all needed to be mourned, dealt with, and healed.

Grieving losses was good for me; I grew deeper in my faith by addressing my losses instead of suppressing them. I needed to feel the pain rather than just push it off or pretend it wasn't real. I needed to cry and mourn because it helped me get in touch with my feelings, even as real, raw, and uncomfortable as they were. It helped me connect with Christ on an emotional level. I felt closer to God because I was completely honest with Him, admitting all the pain I was carrying around from losses. Allowing myself to sit and grieve without any time restrictions was strangely satisfying.

We condition ourselves to cope with loss by shoving it to the back of our minds. We smile through it, dance around it, and laugh to cover it, desperately trying to avoid the painful emotions loss provokes. What we don't do is let the love of Christ into the specific areas of loss in our lives. Thus we remain wounded.

You should pay attention to the emotions you feel after suffering a loss. With life comes loss. Nothing on this earth lasts forever, no matter how much you wish it did. You don't get over the death of someone you love. You don't get over being fired. You don't get over a divorce. You don't get over the death of a dream. So often I hear people advising, "You just need to get over what happened." This is terrible advice, and is actually hurtful instead of helpful.

While the truth is you don't get over losses and sadness, you can get through them, eventually learning to live with a healthy acceptance of them. You can continue to both live and grieve simultaneously. This does not happen overnight, nor does it diminish the pain that accompanies the loss.

This is embracing your humanity. You should grieve loss; actually you *need* to grieve loss. Life is not easy. The road to the grave is littered with loss and all the painful potholes that accompany it. The only recourse is the pot of gold at the end that believers know as heaven.

This is not to say that every day is miserable; many are not. Some days are great. But when loss lingers in your peripheral vision 24/7, it's tough to see those good times with clarity.

What losses have you experienced?

◎ The death of a loved one
◎ Broken relationships
◎ Health problems
◎ Losing a job
◎ Divorce
◎ Unwanted change
◎ A wayward child or children
◎ Kids who grow up too fast
◎ Unmet expectations
◎ An abusive past
◎ Aging parents
◎ Loss of a pet
◎ Community change
◎ Bankruptcy
◎ Other _____

Biblical Heroes Who Grieved Loss

The Bible exposes the emotional state of real people who suffered intense loss. King David spent extended periods of time grieving loss. When his best friend Jonathan died, David mourned his death (see 2 Samuel 1:17–27). He also grieved the broken relationship he had with his rebellious son, Absalom (see 2 Samuel 18:33). The central focus of many of the psalms David wrote is grief, loss, suffering, and sorrow. In Psalm 13:2, David cries out, *"How long must I wrestle with my thoughts and every day have sorrow in my heart?"* The entire psalm speaks about grief, pain, and sorrow until the last verse, which reads, *"I will sing the Lord's praise, for he has been good to me,* (Psalm 13:6).

Jesus grieved loss as well. One clear biblical example of Jesus grieving loss comes from the relationship between Jesus and Lazarus. Jesus was good friends with Lazarus, Mary, and Martha. These were people who were close to Him. Jesus was teaching in Jerusalem when Mary and Martha sent word to Him from the city of Bethany that Lazarus was sick. Lazarus didn't just have a cold; he was dying. Bethany is a mere two miles from Jerusalem, so Jesus could have traveled there in thirty to forty-five minutes if He wanted to. This is what Mary and Martha expected. They expected Jesus to show up when He was needed by them the most. But Jesus didn't come right away. He spent two more days in Jerusalem before traveling the two miles to Bethany to check on Lazarus. In the meantime, Lazarus died. Mary and Martha's friends came to comfort them in their loss. When Jesus stood at the tomb of His dead friend Lazarus, He wept. Why? Because He was grieving the loss of His friend. He could have told everyone to quit crying because He was going to bring Lazarus back from the dead, but He didn't. He stood there with His friends and felt pain from loss. Jesus expressed His emotions through tears of sadness.

On a different occasion, as recorded in Matthew 23:37-39, Jesus openly grieved over the city of Jerusalem because its inhabitants were so far from God. Jesus was emotionally wounded by their hard hearts. The Prophet Isaiah stated hundreds of years before Jesus was even born that He would be a man of sorrows (see Isaiah 53:3). Jesus felt the pain of loss just as you do.

Make an Emotional Connection With Your Losses

Think back over the course of your life. What sadness, grief, sorrow and loss have you experienced? This can be incredibly painful and difficult if you have never thought about all the loss you have experienced. Let the calendar roll back in your mind. What have you lost over the course of your lifetime? What sadness, grief, and sorrow stand out?

- Think back to your childhood. Did a good friend move away? Did someone pass away?

- Did someone abandon you? Did you lose a pet that you loved? Do you mourn the reality that one parent was absent from your life?

- Reflect on your adolescent years. What losses did you experience in junior high? High school? Did a boyfriend or girlfriend break up with you? Did someone close to you betray you? Did your parents get divorced?

- What losses did you experience in college or as a young adult? Did you have any hopes and dreams that died? Do you miss your college friends? Did someone you love die?

You may have lost a parent after a long battle with cancer or in a sudden, tragic car accident. You may have miscarried a child, lost a child, or empathized with a close friend who did. Death is so final, so terminal, so painful. Did you lose a pet that you adored more than anything else? It's okay to miss your pet. It's okay to mourn the loss of life. Allow yourself to go back to the moment when you felt loss.

What Relational Losses Have You Experienced?

Nothing breaks up a family like a divorce. We are not pointing fingers here; we are just mourning the loss of the relationship and the death of a dream. Maybe a friend left you and the wound is still raw. Or, like me, you had a great friend move away, and now there is just a void and a strange family where your best friend used to live.

Have You Experienced the Death of Hopes and Dreams?

Have your kids not lived up to your expectations? They might not talk to you anymore or be involved with someone who is a negative influence. Did you ever lose your job? In today's economy, job loss is common, and it hurts so much. Have you lost your faith? Do you feel that God let you down? You may have been through so much that you stopped praying for yourself. Or you may not believe that God gives a rip anyway because you have not seen God answer any of your prayers.

Loss and sadness are far more present in our lives than we want to admit. Just thinking about loss, sadness, sorrow, and grief hurts. It's okay to feel hurt. It's okay to connect with your emotions. Every loss is different, and so is the pain, but we all feel it. You are not immune to your emotions. You might be good at masking them, cloaking them, hiding them, or ignoring them, but you are not immune to them.

Loss hurts. If we never acknowledge the pain we feel, we will become numb to life itself.

What loss are you still grieving? Can you write it down and articulate it?

Moving From Loss to Life

If you don't learn how to process loss, you will never experience inner peace. You also won't be able to make progress into God's preferred future for you because you will feel stuck, fastened to the past. Loss is unavoidable, and there is emotional cost to every loss. The process of learning how to grieve takes work and transparency, and yet grieving can be very refreshing and beneficial.

- ⊚ Grieving creates a greater dependence on God. You are forced to admit that you cannot control everything.
- ⊚ Grieving helps you be more kind and compassionate to others who are hurting. When you truly allow yourself to feel the emotions pain causes, it makes it a lot easier to empathize and cry with others.
- ⊚ Grieving connects you with your emotions in an authentic way.
- ⊚ Grieving takes away any pretense you have about trying to be perfect. You don't have to fake it anymore.
- ⊚ When you honestly admit that you are hurting, it opens the door for the healing process to begin.
- ⊚ Only after you authentically grieve loss will you be able to express authentic worship.

So how do you move from loss to life? How do you work through the pain of loss when you are not even sure what emotions come with it? By the power of the Holy Spirit, you can grieve loss and reconcile with your emotions. Five steps will help you process the loss in your life so that you can experience a more fulfilling present and even brighter future.

1. Give yourself permission to grieve.

Mary and Martha were grieving. They were mourning their loss, and it hurt. In the same way, you need to give yourself permission to grieve your losses, whether they include the death of a person, the loss of a relationship, or the sadness that some hope or dream died.

When Jesus needed to grieve, He went to be alone and spent

time in prayer. Matthew recorded, *"Then he* [Jesus] *said to them, 'My soul is very sorrowful, even to death; remain here, and watch with me.' And going a little farther he fell on his face and prayed,"* (Matthew 26:38–39).

I have presided over funerals where the spouse of the deceased refused to admit that their husband or wife was dead. Even after a funeral and reading the condolences, the deep pain of loss was too much to bear. Many hopes and dreams had also died with the loved one. There would be no retirement trips to Europe, no long walks, no extra time with the grandkids, no more companionship. With the death, everything had changed, and it was so overwhelming that it was easier to ignore reality.

2. Make an emotional connection with the loss.

Mary, Martha, and Jesus all felt an emotional connection to the loss of Lazarus. They cried over his death. When some people experience a loss, the first thing they may do is run from it and pretend nothing happened. When you experience loss, you need to make an emotional connection with it so you can grieve and thus process your emotions. This is easier if the loss has been more recent, but if you have a lingering loss from the past you can still make an emotional connection with it.

You need to take the time to make an emotional connection with each loss. Trying to process the emotions from all unresolved loss at once is overwhelming and improbable. As you work on processing each loss, ask yourself probing questions like:

- Why do I feel the way I do about this loss?
- Why don't I feel anything related to this?
- Do I feel angry? Sad? Confused?
- Am I upset because I don't have any answers?

Grief can trigger many different and unexpected emotions, including denial, anger, bargaining, and depression. When you experience loss, you should allow yourself to experience the feelings that come with it. God wants us to be in touch with our feelings, or we will always live our lives in the shallow end of the pool. Joy, grief, and sadness are all God-given emotions that add color and depth to life.

3. Surrender the sadness from loss to Jesus.

When Jesus did arrive in Bethany, Mary was crushed and said, "Lord, if you had been here, my brother would not have died" (John 11:20). She felt sadness because Lazarus was dead and was assertive with Jesus because she knew He could have prevented it. She knew He was the Messiah and she still felt let down by Him because He didn't show up when she thought He should have. Martha's response to the situation reveals her heart and ultimately that she was willing to surrender the situation to God.

She said what we often think. *Where were you, God? Where were you when mom died? Where were you when I was in the middle of the divorce? Where were you, God, when I needed you most?* It's okay to tell God you are upset. It is okay to cry out to God and let Him know how you really feel. After Martha told Jesus she wished He had come earlier, she confessed that she believed He is the Messiah. This is when she surrendered the sadness to Jesus, *"Yes, Lord," she replied, "I believe that you are the Messiah, the Son of God, who is to come into the world,"* (John 11:27).

Martha is affirming her faith in the middle of her misery. She knew she could surrender the sadness to Jesus. It helps to surrender the sadness to the only One who can truly absorb it.

The Scriptures state that the Lord is close to the brokenhearted. The psalmist wrote, *"The Lord is close to the brokenhearted and saves those who are crushed in spirit,"* (Psalm 34:11).

When I was brokenhearted, grieving the losses in my life, I felt the presence of God more than I have felt it in a long time. It was as if the Holy Spirit was filling all the holes loss had left in my life. The holes were still there, but the grace of God was filling the void. The wounds had begun to heal. The same is true for you. When you surrender the sadness to Jesus, He will fill the gap with His grace in a supernatural way by the power of the Holy Spirit, if you let Him.

4. Allow the Holy Spirit to work in the wound.

Jesus, Martha, Mary, and others all went to Lazarus' tomb to grieve. Verses 33–35 read as follows, *"When Jesus saw her weeping, and the Jews who had come along with her also weeping, he was deeply moved in spirit and troubled. 'Where have you laid him?' he asked. 'Come and see, Lord,' they replied. Jesus wept,"* (John 11:33–35). Seeing His friends Mary and Martha so brokenhearted broke Jesus' heart, too. Could He have come earlier and spared Lazarus the agony of death? Sure, but He didn't. He came in His divine timing. Mary and Martha spent time grieving with Jesus. In the same way, we need to spend time with Jesus, grieving, and allow the Holy Spirit to work in the wound.

How do you let God work in your wounds? Spend time in prayer, talking to God about the wounds you have. I like to talk out loud to God when I am alone. I also like to read the psalms. When a passage sticks out to me, I pause and read it through again, letting it soak in and asking God what He wants me to learn. God often places passages on my heart that reveal work I need to do in a specific area related to the loss. Let God work in the wound. Let Him into your pain and loss. God will be with you in your sadness and loss. People without any faith won't understand how God can comfort in times of crisis. They just don't get it, and can't get it, because their hope only exists in what they can see and do themselves.

You also need to be transparent and authentic with a good friend. Talk to a trusted friend who is a believer and is willing to listen. Your friend does not need to have all the answers, and you might even want to tell the person that. Just ask your friend to listen to your heart and empathize with your emotions. Seek out face-to-face support from people who care about you. You can't do this via text or e-mail; it has to be face to face. Over the years, I have learned that in times of deep loss, people don't desire advice; they simply want you to be present. Often the best thing you can do for someone who is grieving is to be near them and care about them. People don't always want advice, but they do want someone to hold their hand, hug them, and cry with them.

5. Embrace the hope God has for you.

After Lazarus died, his friends wrapped his body in cloth and spices, which was customary at the time. Lazarus wasn't just in a coma or sleeping; he was dead. His tomb was carved out of stone in a rock wall, like a cave. He had been in the tomb for four days. By the time Jesus and the others got there, his body would have started to decompose. That is why Martha hesitated when Jesus asked for the stone to be rolled away. What happens next is one of the greatest miracles ever recorded. Jesus prayed to His heavenly Father and commanded Lazarus to come back to life, and he did.

Lazarus walked out of the tomb wrapped in the grave clothes. Many people witnessed this and put their faith in trust in Jesus.

In the same way, if you believe, God will resurrect hope within you even after you have suffered significant loss. Life will never be the same, and you will never forget what happened, but God can fill in the holes with His grace so you can live again.

Personal Exercise

Take a blank sheet of paper and write "Dear God," at the top. Then write a letter to Him. Write to God about the loss you have experienced in your life. Write down your feelings and emotions that run parallel with the loss. This is a very personal exercise that will help you to process the loss in your life. Do it when you are ready and are willing to be transparent with God. Don't rush the experience; let it happen in one sitting, with plenty of margin. Don't skip this step. You may have buried your pain so deeply or avoided it for so long that it's going to be really hard to embrace it, work through it, and be freed from it. Take all the time you need, and you will be better for it. May you come to the point when you can honestly say, "I will sing to the Lord for he has been good to me," just like David did after he finished grieving.

God's hope is available for you to have; you just need to reach out and grab it. You need to hold God's hand and walk with Him hour after hour and day by day, claiming His promises recorded in the Bible.

God's has promised to be with you. The following Scripture verses confirm this. Which ones stand out to you as you read them?

God is our refuge and strength, an ever-present help in trouble. (Psalm 46:1)

Have I not commanded you? Be strong and courageous. Do not be afraid; do not be discouraged, for the Lord your God will be with you wherever you go. (Joshua 1:9)

"For I know the plans I have for you," declares the Lord, "plans to prosper you and not to harm you, plans to give you hope and a future." (Jeremiah 29:11)

"Though the mountains be shaken and the hills be removed, yet my unfailing love for you will not be shaken nor my covenant of peace be removed," says the Lord, who has compassion on you. (Isaiah 54:10)

The Lord is my shepherd, I lack nothing. He makes me lie down in green pastures, he leads me beside quiet waters, he refreshes my soul. He guides me along the right paths for his name's sake. Even though I walk through the darkest valley, I will fear no evil, for you are with me; your rod and your staff, they comfort me. (Psalm 23:1–4)

Therefore, since we have been justified through faith, we have peace with God through our Lord Jesus Christ, through whom we have gained access by faith into this grace in which we now stand. And we boast in the hope of the glory of God. Not only so, but we also glory in our sufferings, because we know that suffering produces perseverance; perseverance, character; and character, hope. And hope does not put us to shame, because God's love has been poured out into our hearts through the Holy Spirit, who has been given to us. (Romans 5:1–5)

But we have this treasure in jars of clay to show that this all-surpassing power is from God and not from us. We are hard pressed on every side, but not crushed; perplexed, but not in despair; persecuted, but not abandoned; struck down, but not destroyed. (2 Corinthians 4:7–9)

Ultimately, believers have hope to heal from all past wounds and present circumstances. The future promises resurrection. One day, believers will be reunited with their loved ones who also had faith in Christ. They will be with God, basking in His radiant love where there is no sorrow, sadness, or loss. But until that day comes, we must cling to the hope God gives us here and now.

God is able to help you in your crisis. God is able to heal your broken heart. He is able to fill in the holes. God can resurrect your faith. Let God minister to you in your misery. Let Him into your life.

What Does Healing From Loss Feel Like?

Loss always leaves a scar, but it doesn't hurt as it once did. Loss can lead to a closer intimacy with Christ. Loss can also lead to something new that you cannot see yet. It may be a new opportunity, a new dream, a deeper understanding, or appreciation for life itself. God will never waste your pain. He will never waste a hurt. He can and will use your situation to help others. Paul wrote,

> *Praise be to the God and Father of our Lord Jesus Christ, the Father of compassion and the God of all comfort, who comforts us in all our troubles, so that we can comfort those in any trouble with the comfort we ourselves receive from God.* (2 Corinthians 1:3–4)

You will know that you are experiencing healing from loss when the wounds start to heal and scar over. Each and every scar has a story and pain attached to it, but it isn't an open wound anymore. You will always remember the loss that caused the scar, but you don't have to cover it up and pretend it isn't there anymore. Your life will never be the same again, but that doesn't mean that your life is over.

Loss leaves scars but they can feel different. Describing how one feels after processing loss is difficult to put into words, but I do know that you know will when you are healing. This is how you might describe what it feels like to heal from loss:

> *Like a warm comforter on a cold day.*
>
> *Like a new spring after a cold, intense winter.*
>
> *Like a fresh rain after a serious drought.*
>
> *Like soft music that comforts.*
>
> *Like the sweet sound of silence.*
>
> *Like the smile on your face when you see a rainbow.*
>
> *Like the fluffy feel of fine cashmere.*
>
> *Like the smell of fresh-cut flowers.*
>
> *Like comfortable shoes.*
>
> *Like a familiar sweatshirt.*
>
> *Like the warm rays of the sun.*
>
> *Like a new day dawning.*

Your scars from loss are part of your unique story, something to be processed and accepted because the only other option is continued pain and hurt. Wounds from loss take a long period of time to heal. They won't heal overnight, or even in a week or two, because they are deep, difficult, and hard to touch. Sometimes that wound will start to hurt over again, but it will hurt less if you have processed the loss.

The apostle Paul knew what it meant to suffer loss and finish strong. God inspired him to write,

But we have this treasure in jars of clay to show that this all-surpassing power is from God and not from us. We are hard pressed on every side, but not crushed; perplexed, but not in despair; persecuted, but not abandoned; struck down, but not destroyed. (2 Corinthians 4:7–9)

The power to heal from and through loss comes from God. You may be hard-pressed right now, but you are not crushed. You may be perplexed as to why all this happened, but you don't have to be in despair. God is with you. You may be persecuted, but you are not abandoned. You may be struck down, but you are not destroyed. You can mourn loss and still experience life.

At the end of the first day at the ranch, all I had managed to do was write down all of the loss I have felt in my life, and it was more than enough. For the first time I can remember, I let myself cry over all the pain and feel my own emotions. Since I was all alone, I didn't have to fake my emotions or cover them in any way. And once I became vulnerable, God showed up and moved in me. In a crazy strange way, God showed up in my pain and loss and brought me hope and healing. God's love seeped into the holes of loss, filling them with His presence. The view of the mountains brought me a new sense of joy and peace that I had never been able to perceive before.

My hope for you is that today God will help you to process and heal from your loss. Your feelings are real and painful, and they also need to be processed. The Holy Spirit will show up in your loss and help you heal the wounds, turning them into scars that are part of your life story. With God's help you can move through your loss and experience life again. Your life will never be the same, but there will be more life to live.

CHAPTER 7

HEALTHY RHYTHMS

The speaker at the conference I was attending was passionate, articulate, and convinced that everyone could and should live a balanced life. With charts and graphs, he explained exactly what living a balanced life looked like. He made it sound so simple and achievable. After his session, I was convinced that living a balanced life could be done with enough discipline, effort, and determination. Essentially, the motivated speaker said that a balanced life consisted of three parts:

- Eight hours sleeping
- Eight hours with family
- Eight hours working

He subdivided these master categories to incorporate daily exercise, eating three balanced meals per day, spending equal time with each family member, and a bunch of other things I can't remember. On the surface, the balanced life argument made sense. After all, living a balanced life is what everyone seems to be striving for; a plethora of self-help books certainly push it. Who wants to live a lopsided life or an out-of-balance life? Books about that kind of life don't sell and never will.

For a season, I tried all the tricks I learned at the seminar to live a balanced life. The first day, I had a crisis that pushed my daily office workday into the early evening. That shortchanged the time I had allotted for my kids and cascaded into my wife's special time. I had planned to get eight hours of sleep, but that didn't work out so well either. (There was a must-see TV program on that night.) The next day was equally deplorable. I managed to work for only eight hours and spent four or five hours with my family. But we skipped the balanced meal for fast food, and one of our kids needed help with homework. Day two ended completely lopsided. Days three, four, and five were just as scattered. After five days of effort, all I felt was intense guilt for failing to live a balanced life.

The Myth of Living a Balanced Life

Living a balanced life sounds good in theory, but in reality, it's impossible. Trust me, I really tried to do it and failed miserably. I found it nearly impossible to eat balanced meals at ideal times every day. I could not balance my marriage, family, work, relationships, and unexpected interruptions with pinpoint discipline every day, and neither can you, so let's stop trying. Gymnasts, bikers, and tightrope walkers need balance. And unless you are doing one of these activities right now, your goal should not be balance; it should be understanding and leveraging your natural life rhythms.

In other words, the secret to life isn't balance; it's finding and understanding your life rhythm and learning how to live in harmony with it. Learning to live within the natural cycles of your life rhythm is achievable, and once you understand your rhythms you can work in sync with them instead of fighting against them. This will give you less guilt and more peace, lower stress and greater fulfillment. You will feel less fragmented and more contented. You won't just be surviving; you can actually be thriving. By rejecting the pursuit of living some elusive "balanced life," you will free yourself from impossible expectations and unrealistic goals, enabling you to be at peace with the pace of your life.

King Solomon wrote about living a rhythmic life:
There is a time for everything,
and a season for every activity under the heavens:
a time to be born and a time to die,
a time to plant and a time to uproot,
a time to kill and a time to heal,
a time to tear down and a time to build,
a time to weep and a time to laugh,
a time to mourn and a time to dance,
a time to scatter stones and a time to gather them,
a time to embrace and a time to refrain from embracing,
a time to search and a time to give up,
a time to keep and a time to throw away,
a time to tear and a time to mend,
a time to be silent and a time to speak,
a time to love and a time to hate,
a time for war and a time for peace. (Ecclesiastes 3:1–8)
Solomon is speaking about rhythm, not balance. He never advises spending eight hours doing this and eight hours doing

that. He makes no mention of keeping track of what you eat and when you eat it. His focus is on understanding that life ebbs and flows. In other words, your life has a rhythm to it, and once you understand your rhythm you can learn how to make the most of it.

Chronos and Kairos Time

The ancient Greeks had two words for time, *chronos* and *kairos*. *Chronos* refers to chronological or sequential time. *Chronos* time is quantitative in nature. It has predictable cycles. There are five *chronos* cycles of time.

Yearly—365 days

Quarterly—4 quarters

Monthly—12 months

Weekly—7 days

Daily—24 hours

A picture of a calendar best represents *chronos* time:

Chronos time is easily measurable because it occurs in known cycles. We put special dates on the calendar because they are predictable. We can count the number of days until they arrive or since they have passed. Christmas is on December 25th every year. In the United States, Independence Day (the "Fourth of July") is on the July 4th. Your birthday is on the same date every year. It might be a Saturday one year and a Tuesday in another year, but the date itself does not change. *Chronos* time is constant and universal. It is quantifiable, a physical concept. Plato and Aristotle linked *chronos* time with movement and change. Solomon was speaking of *chronos* time in when he wrote, *"a time to be born and a time to die, a time to plant and a time to uproot."* *Chronos* time is referred to fifty-four times in the New Testament when specific units of time are mentioned, such as "a day" or "an hour" (see, for example, Acts 13:18 and 27:9).

The Sabbath is part of the *chronos* cycle of time. Work for six days then take one day of rest and worship. We all have daily cycles such as eating breakfast in the morning, lunch at midday, and dinner in the early evening. Keeping a regular exercise schedule or a Bible-reading schedule, or even taking medications at certain times of the day—all are examples of how we use *chronos* time to build routine into our lives.

Kairos is an ancient Greek word meaning the right, critical, or opportune moment. *Kairos* is qualitative time rather than quantitative, and it is linked to one's personal seasons and stages of life. Personal seasons and life stages ebb and flow as one's circumstances change. In the New Testament, *kairos* means "the appointed time in the purpose of God," the time when God acts (see Mark 1:15). *Kairos* time is referred to eighty-six times in the New Testament in the context of opportune times (a moment or a season such as "harvest time").

Two Types of Kairos Time

Kairos time can be defined in two different ways, by a person's stage of life and maturity or by the seasons of a person's life, which are unique to each person.

1. Stage of life. The first type of *kairos* time is based on one's life stage. Life stages are universal to all people because everyone experiences them, although their chronology may differ from person to person. For example, childhood is a life stage because you are only a child once and you grow out of childhood. Adolescence is a life stage you also grow into and out of. Exactly when childhood stops and adolescence begins is hard to pin down because it's different for everyone; there is no specific day that a person transitions from childhood to adolescence. Some twelve-year-olds act like adolescents, while other sixteen-year-olds still act like children. Adulthood is a stage with many of its own stages, from young adulthood through mature adulthood. College could be considered a life stage of young adulthood, whether a person goes through college right after high school or takes a year or two off first. Everybody's experience is different. Some get married; some don't. Some have children; some don't. Some have steady careers, while others jump from job to job or struggle with unemployment. All of it is part of adulthood. Retirement is a life stage. Some people retire at 62 and others at 72. These life stages are experienced at different chronological (*chronos*) times by every individual.

When Solomon wrote of *"a time to weep and a time to laugh, a time to mourn and a time to dance,"* he was writing about life stages, *kairos* time.

2. **Personal seasons.** The second type of *kairos* time is based on one's personal seasons. Personal seasons are identified by significant experiences one has. Personal seasons are similar to weather seasons like spring, summer, fall, and winter. These seasons are experienced multiple times over the course of one's life. Personal seasons include events such as recovering from an injury, dealing with the loss of a job, or mourning the absence of a good friend. Other examples of personal seasons include times of intense busyness, sadness, joy, abundance, or monotony. Some personal seasons are restful and relaxing, like a warm summer day, others are taxing and tiring, like getting a flat tire on a bitter-cold Minnesota winter's night. A personal season may involve the excitement of landing a better job or be experienced in a sudden shift in your financial status. These personal seasons are not necessarily predictable.

Ignoring Your Kairos Rhythms Leads to Frustration

Deep down inside, I have always had a desire to please people, which is not necessarily a bad thing. I try to get along with others and to love them as Jesus would (though I'm not successful at it all the time). Because I want to please people, I have a tendency to overcommit myself. Consistently overcommitting oneself tends to drain life of joy, pleasure, and purpose. I ended up feeling guilty for not spending enough time with my children and guilty for not helping everyone who asks for help at church.

I needed to adjust to the season of life I was in. In reality, parenting young children takes an enormous amount of time. I was depleted by my poor decision to not accept my stage of life as a young parent along with my season of life as a pastor of a very active, young church. My exhaustion was evident in my poor attitude, short temper, and internalized anger, which seeped out onto my family and close friends.

I was not happy; I was miserable. I was letting other people control my calendar, and unwittingly, they were draining the life out of me. It was like death by a thousand paper cuts. I had to accept the reality that with kids at home and a growing church to lead I could not be at every event and do every wedding. I had to establish some boundaries. I needed to care for my own kids and invest in my marriage, and this involved putting my family first on my priority list. It's not that I stopped loving others or investing in them, but I had to accept my own stage and season of life.

There will be times in your life when you need to step up and get more involved and times you need to step away, allowing someone else to take the lead or volunteer. Identifying what life stage or season you are in will help you make important decisions surrounding how you use your time, whether you're talking about *chronos* time or *kairos* time.

Time Management

In order to understand your life rhythms, you need to account for where your time goes. If I were to follow you around and observe you for a week, I could tell you where you spend your time. You might not like or agree with my observations, but I would be right. Your calendar may not reflect your actual priorities, only what you'd like them to be. Your calendar might show your appointments and commitments, but it won't show your social media usage or the time you spend watching YouTube or traditional TV Everyone has the same number of hours in each day but the time is not spent in the same ways by all. Where does all that time go?

Author Steven Covey developed what is called the time management matrix. It identifies four quadrants people spend their time in. Every activity that you do fits into one of four quadrants. If you do an honest assessment of your life's primary activities and plot them on the matrix, it will help you see where all of your time goes. Covey's time quadrant can be eye-opening.[26]

	URGENT	NOT URGENT
IMPORTANT	QUADRANT I **EMERGENCIES** • Crises • Illness/Injuries • Deadline-driven projects • Last-minute details for scheduled activities • Pressing problems	QUADRANT II **QUALITY ACTIVITIES** • Relationship building • Activity preparation/planning • Exercise • Recreation • Education • Prevention
NOT IMPORTANT	QUADRANT III **DISTRACTIONS** • Interruptions • Most emails • Most phone calls • Some meetings • Some reports	QUADRANT IV **TIME WASTERS** • Busy work • Some email • Some phone calls • Mindless TV shows • Escape activities • Most social media

The things that fill Quadrant I are the activities that are urgent and important. Pretty much any major crisis or pressing problem falls into the urgent-important quadrant. Your baby with a poopy diaper will scream and scream until you change it. Just about everything in Quadrant I has an instant payoff. The kids stops screaming, the cut stops bleeding, the dog stops barking. We like these kinds of problems because, when we solve them, we get repaid for doing it.

---

26   Adapted from *7 Habits of Highly Effective People* by Stephen Covey.

Quadrant II is filled with the activities that are not urgent but important. For example, when you go to the doctor for a checkup, you are doing something that is important and not urgent. And when you change your oil, you are doing something that is important but not urgent. You can go over by a few hundred miles between changes without your car blowing up. It's very important but it's not urgent. Spending time with family is important but usually not urgent. Going to church or participating in a small group are important things but not urgent. And most of the time there is no instant payoff for Quadrant II activities. The reward will come later, sometimes much later.

Quadrant III is filled with activities that are not important but urgent. Most phone calls, text messages, and even social media updates fall into this quadrant. You can be right in the middle of a tense conversation with someone, and when the phone rings, you answer it with a pleasant "Hello." Why? Because at the moment, answering the phone was a priority. Most of the time, it's nothing urgent, but when that phone rings, people treat it as urgent no matter who is calling.

Quadrant IV activities are the things that are neither urgent nor important, but we still do them. Checking your Facebook status or thumbing through Instagram or Snapchat falls into this category. Nobody is going to die if you don't check your Facebook status; you just do it. There's nothing bad about playing games like Farmville or Mafia Wars, but nothing important either. Quadrant IV is where our leisure activities fall.

So where do most people spend their time? They spend it in Quadrants I and IV. Yet, if you want to make the most of your time and grow as a person, you need to invest your time in Quadrant II activities. These are the activities that deepen life. If you want to reach any of your life goals, you need to spend time with your family, attend church, participate in a small group, serve others, invest in friendships, and the like. The problem is, most Quadrant II activities get crowded out by the activities of other quadrants.

Jesus was incredibly busy. People were all over Him all the time, yet He still found time to invest in His disciples. He still took time to go away and pray. The New Testament gives at least six specific incidents when Jesus retreated to pray. He invested His time in pursuing His priorities (see Luke 6:12–19).

Jesus lived His life in rhythm with his priorities. He taught the masses then retreated with His friends. He was close to all twelve disciples but especially close to only three. Jesus understood *chronos* rhythms because He participated in the Jewish calendar, celebrating the feasts, honoring the Sabbath, and sleeping and waking just like everybody else. He also understood *kairos* rhythms. He took time to rest before and after big events. On one occasion, Jesus taught the masses, then got into a boat and traveled across the Sea of Galilee. He was exhausted from speaking, so He needed to rest, and the boat ride offered Him time to rest. Jesus understood how to use both *chronos* time and *kairos* time for the greatest effectiveness and for His own well-being.

Before Jesus was to die on the cross, He needed solitude and rest. He knew that He was going to suffer immense pain and agony on the cross, so He took His close friends and went to a quiet place to get prepared.

They went to a place called Gethsemane, and Jesus said to his disciples, "Sit here while I pray." He took Peter, James and John along with him, and he began to be deeply distressed and troubled. (Mark 14:32–33)

His goal was not contentment but obedience. You will always find that an obedient life is a life lived in rhythm and harmony with *chronos* time and *kairos* time. Jesus managed His time well. You need to do the same. Look for opportunities when you can manage your time better by saying "no." Don't feel guilty because you can't do everything. Set yourself free by understanding your own *chronos* and *kairos* rhythms and learning to live within them. You will be much happier if you do.

How to Get in Sync With Your Life Rhythms

Take time to evaluate your life so you can get in sync with your life rhythms.

1. Identify the stage of life you are in.

It is easy to identify the stage of life you are in. Are you single? Preparing to get married? Expecting a child? Raising young children? Sending your child or children off to college? Are you preparing to retire or enter the workforce? Take an honest assessment of the stage of life you are in right now. Identify it and write it down.

2. Identify the season of life you are in.

If you just had a baby, chances are that you are not going to be able to go to the gym every day, have coffee with friends, stay up late, and maintain your career at the same level you did previously. You won't be able to go shopping all day just to relax and unwind. Taking kids to the mall is torture; as I know from experience.

If you are stressing because you can't do it all, set yourself free from unrealistic expectations by radically accepting the season of life you are in right now. If you have small children, your house will be full of toys, and the yard might get neglected. It will not look like your retired neighbor's, no matter how much you or they think it should. If he wants your yard to look like his, then ask him to mow it. After all, are you raising kids or raising grass? Teenagers' cars may clutter up your driveway. The laundry room might not ever be featured on HGTV. Be okay with it; this is the season of life you are in right now.

Ask yourself: What season of life am I in right now? How do I feel? (Overwhelmed. Exhausted. Tired. Blah. OK. Fair. Content. Hopeful. Energized...)

3. Recognize when your kairos rhythms have shifted.

Your *kairos* rhythms will shift as your seasons and stages of life change. When friends found out their teen daughter was pregnant, they were devastated. For years they had looked forward to being empty-nesters so they could travel and spend more time cultivating relationships. But their daughter's pregnancy changed everything. She was in high school and would not be able to support herself and the baby. Her pregnancy had cascading ramifications for her parents and siblings. Instead of taking a vacation during the summer, her father spent the vacation money he had saved on remodeling a room for the baby. After the baby was born, they felt that they had to stay home to help out where they could. Raising a child is difficult enough; raising a teenager with a child adds three times the complexity and ten times the stress. Once the parents accepted the abrupt change to their life stage, their stress level dropped and their joy returned. But it took a long time for them to come to a radical acceptance of the situation.

The most content people in life understand what season of life they are in and embrace that stage. When I had to carry my infant children around in a car seat, I could not wait for them to start to crawl. Then, once they started to crawl, I wished they were back in the car seat so I could always know where they were. At the time, I didn't understand or accept my season of life as it related to theirs, and it always created a level of discontent in my life. I wished my son were an inch taller so we could ride the big rides at the fair. I wished my daughter could have played with the older and more-skilled girls in hockey. I wanted my youngest to start school later because I enjoyed having her home. I was always busy wishing they were in some other stage, and it robbed me of the joy I could have been experiencing if I would have simply lived in harmony with the moment.

What expectations have you put on yourself that are unrealistic? Could it be that some of the things you want to do today are really meant for a different season of life? If they are, let them go for now. Embrace the season of life you are in now rather than mourning a season that isn't yours right now.

What *kairos* shift has taken place in your life that you need to embrace?

Has your family situation shifted?

_____

_____

_____

Have your energy levels shifted? How so?

_____

_____

_____

Has your career shifted demanding more or less from you?

_____

---

4. Plan *chronos* rhythms that enhance your life.

Pace yourself and build rituals and routines into your life that make your life better—the sooner you do this, the better. One of the rituals I have built into my life is taking a Sabbath day to rest and worship. I never used to take a day off at all, and I was breaking the fourth commandment.[27]

I also built certain routines into my life. One of my favorite routines is to have coffee with friends. I have had coffee with Bob and Georgean at their home once a week for over twenty-four years. I go there because it's something I really enjoy. I also have lunch with a good friend almost every Wednesday, unless one of us is traveling. He runs a bustling company yet makes time to meet every week because this routine enhances our lives.

Developing healthy *chronos* rhythms may require some out-of-the-box thinking. When my kids were all in school, for a time I was frustrated because our family didn't get to spend as much time together as we used to. So I decided to change our routine. I started getting up early and making breakfast for them instead of expecting everyone to be home for dinner. This was very beneficial. I had wasted three years feeling guilty for not living a balanced family life. All I did was start one new healthy ritual, and it changed everything. Figure out your life rhythm and build rituals that give life.

When our children were young, we didn't have money for big vacations, but we still planned simple weekend getaways. One time, we took our kids to a hotel just thirty minutes away from

---

27 Remember the Sabbath day, to keep it holy.

our home for a vacation. To them, the thirty-minute drive felt like they were going to the other end of the world. That was all we could afford at that season in our lives. We ate pizza, popcorn, and chips, and we stayed up late watching cartoons. In the morning, we went for another swim in the pool before heading "all the way home." They loved it, and so did Kathi and I.

You also need to plan times of rest in your schedule. Oscillate between work and rest depending on your *kairos* rhythms. There are times in life when we need to dig in, stay late, and get the job done. Other times we need to come home early or take a nap because we are tired. Do you need more work or more rest right now?

The key is to plan events in your life that match your stage of life and personal season of life. This will make life more enjoyable for you. The added benefit of living within your rhythms is others around you will also be affected because you won't be so crabby all the time. Rather than complaining about what you can't do because you don't have enough time or money, focus on what you can do with what you have in this particular period on your life. Learn to pace yourself. Release yourself from unrealistic expectations, and you will be so much happier.

The concept of rhythm makes sense and is achievable, whereas the concept of balance sounds good but falls flat when examined through a realistic lens. Solomon said, *"There is a time for everything, and a season for every activity under the heavens,"* (Ecclesiastes 3:1). This verse speaks to the practicality of living a rhythmic life.

5. Ask a trusted friend to help you discern your rhythms.

Everyone has blind spots, which is why they are called blind spots. You need another person to point out your blind spots.

Ask a friend to help you see them. "Do I seem to be too busy or too hurried? Do you think I spend enough time taking care of myself? Or do I possibly focus too much on myself?" It's easy to deceive yourself into thinking you are in harmony with your *kairos* rhythms when in reality you are not.

A few years ago Kathi, and I went out for dinner with my friend and mentor, Leith Anderson, and his wife, Charleen. During our conversation, I humbly confessed to him that my out-of-control schedule was starting to wear on me. I had too much to do and couldn't keep up. At the time, Leith was the head of the National Association of Evangelicals, leader of a megachurch, author of a weekly column for *The Washington Post*, host of a weekly radio program, and wrote consistently for many other publications. Leith was a very busy man with a rigorous schedule, yet he seemed calm.

After listening to me for a minute or two, he looked at me right in the eye and said, "John, who controls your schedule?"

"I do."

"Then," he said, "fix it." That was it; that was his advice, plain and simple. As the one in control of my schedule, I was the one who needed to fix it. So I started to figure out where all of my time goes, and to do that I had to think long and hard about my priorities.

Clearly, Leith understood his own *chronos* and *kairos* rhythms. He had great staff working for him, and all of his children were grown and living on their own. In that season of his life, he was able to write, travel, and manage a very heavy workload. When his kids were little, he did not carry the same workload.

Whatever you prioritize will always be evident on your calendar, in your finances, and in your relationships because your priorities leave fingerprints all over your life. What are your priorities right now? Do you know? I'm not asking you about your intentions. What are you actually prioritizing? I'm convinced that most people have lingering feelings of guilt because their stated priorities don't line up with what they actually prioritize.

For example, most parents say they prioritize their kids, but in reality, they spend far less time with them than they think. According to studies, moms spent an average of 104 minutes per day on childcare activities. And dads spend an average of only 59 minutes per day with their kids.[28] If you desire to spend more time with your family, prioritize them in your schedule. Same goes for all of your significant relationships, exercise routine, and time with God.

You will be much more satisfied if you set your priorities based on your chronos *and* kairos *rhythms.*

Study after study confirms that people who prioritize family and friends are much happier than those who don't. If this is true, and I believe the data is correct, then why don't people schedule more time to be with their family and friends? And when it comes to prioritizing your faith, 45 percent of people who attend a religious service weekly say they are "very happy," while only 28 percent of those who never attend said the same.[29] If this is true, why don't people prioritize going to church to worship with others, cultivating their spiritual life and connection to others?

---

28   May, Ashley. "Study: Parents Spend More Time with Children Now than They Did 50 Years Ago." USA Today. October 01, 2016. Accessed August 13, 2018. https://www.usatoday.com/story/news/nation-now/2016/09/30/parents-spend-more-time-children-now-than-they-did-50-years-ago/91263880.

29   Adams, Charlene. "Religious People Much Happier and Have More 'life Satisfaction' than Others, Study Finds." Daily Mail Online. December 25, 2014. Accessed April 13, 2018. http://www.dailymail.co.uk/news/article-2886974/Study-Religious-people-happier-life-satisfaction-others.html#ixzz4mji3cxoY.

If you are single, enjoy this stage and season of your life. If you are just starting your career, enjoy it. If you have young kids at home, enjoy rocking them to sleep and feeding them with a spoon. Stop wishing they were older or younger, or this or that. In ten years, your kids will be young adults. You don't want to look back with regrets, wishing you had spent more time with them. There will be plenty of time in the next season of your life to work outside the home, work more hours, or manicure your lawn. Your kids will only play T-ball for a time, and they will only be in so many school sing-alongs. Enjoy each and every one of them. Seize the moments of time that bring you life. You will only have a few years to raise your kids. When your child scores a goal, celebrate the moment in time and remember it. You will forget what day it happened on, but you will never forget what the moment felt like.

Eat lunch with your child at school. Go on a date together. Recognize and embrace the life stage and personal season you are in. Your daughter will only want to be seen with you in public for so long (trust me, I know). Your parents are still interested in your life; you need to be interested in theirs. If your mom or dad live close, take them out for dinner or call them just to say, "Hi." Seize the season you are in now.

If you are retired and enjoy traveling, go for it. Spend time with friends; volunteer now as much as you wish you could have years ago. Invest in the next generation. Don't judge your neighbor with young kids for mowing the lawn once a month when you have the time to mow three times a week. You are in a different season of life than they are. Accept it and embrace it—and maybe even volunteer to mow their lawn a couple times to help lighten their load. Doing so will give you a fresh sense of joy and freedom.

How much better would your life be if you actually prioritized what you really value? I have a pretty good idea. For starters, you would feel less guilt and more joy. And you would feel less stressed and more energized. T en years from now you would look back and feel a sense of accomplishment because you lived in harmony with your season and stage of life. I don't want to live a life filled with good intentions. I want to live a full life with no regrets. I know that you do too.

CHAPTER 8

SOUL CARE

Philosophers have debated the meaning of "soul" for centuries. Your soul isn't a little thing that resides between your heart and lungs. Your soul isn't something that can be stolen or removed from your physical body either. Your soul is "the immaterial essence, animating principle, or actuating cause of your life."[30] Your soul is the essence of who you are, your total self. Christians believe the Bible teaches that the soul is immortal and therefore will go to heaven (or hell) after a person's physical body ceases to function.

The journey from wounded to wonderful includes learning to care for your own soul, your very essence. You must learn how to care for your soul because you are the only one who can. I am not talking about salvation here, so don't label me a heretic. I believe

---

30 "Soul," Mirriam-Webster.com, 2019 (https://www.merriam-webster.com/dictionary/soul), accessed January 19, 2019.

God is the judge and that salvation can only come through faith in Jesus Christ. But in a more practical application of the meaning of soul, you are the only one who can care for the essence of you. Others can offer advice and assistance, but you are ultimately the only one who can care for yourself.

Seven overarching areas of life culminate in the broader concept of caring for your soul. They are:

1. BUILD healthy margins into your life.
2. ENGAGE your emotions.
3. CARE for your physical body.
4. PRIORITIZE life-giving relationships.
5. MANAGE your finances well.
6. ENJOY ample recreation.
7. FILL your spirit.

When you neglect to care for your soul, the evidence accumulates quickly. You hurt yourself and others close to you. You may damage your reputation and your future. You may harbor deep resentment against others and walk around angry all the time. You may overwork because it's easier to work harder and longer than to face the real problem. You might lose focus, miss deadlines, leave a string of projects undone, or even forget family or social commitments.

Once you start to neglect your soul, you will try to cope with the pain in some other way so you can still feel good. Some people cope by escaping. They watch hours and hours of TV, YouTube, or Netflix. They spend untold hours gaming or surfing the web. Others self-medicate with alcohol, drugs, food, or even over-exercising. Many turn to pornography or isolate themselves. Some people spend money like crazy because it triggers a release of endorphins and gives them feelings of euphoria and freedom. But these feelings are short-lived, often causing financial problems that lead to even more stress. When your soul is drained, it affects everything.

The good news is that you can change. You can care for your soul. Pastor Andy Stanley preached a sermon series titled "Breathing Room." He opened the series by asking what I thought was a profound question, "Do you want to reorganize your life, or do you want to revolutionize your life?" The truth is, most of the information you think will help you, actually only focuses on reorganizing your life, not revolutionizing it. If all you want to do is reorganize your life, here are a few tips:

- Organize your closet.
- Buy all the same type and color of socks.
- Pay with cash as much as you can.
- Use only one credit card.
- Give away any clothing you have not worn for six months.
- Don't shop unless you need something.
- Limit your social media time.
- Live within your means.

These are good tips, and if you want to reorganize your life pick a couple off the list to do this week. When people start to unclutter their lives, they almost always start by creating a new "to do" list and making a halfhearted commitment; I know I do. Who doesn't need to clean out closets or reorganize the living room once in a while?

But if you really want to revolutionize how you live, think, and act, you need to start caring for your soul. You can do this, and here is how.

Build Healthy Margins Into Your Life

My parents noticed I was stressed all the time because of my busy schedule. In their subtle, nice, Minnesota way, they gave me a hint something needed to change. They gave me a very nice analog desk clock made out of wood with a classy face on it. Engraved in the wood below the clock face is a quote from Golda Meir that reads, "I must govern the clock, not be governed by it." They didn't have to say a word; I got the point.

There is a big difference between being lazy and recharging. American culture values busyness and unwittingly affirms that if you aren't busy, you're lazy. But is this accurate? Do you always have to be busy to be valuable? No, absolutely not. You don't have to schedule every minute of every day with everything under the sun. If you don't control your schedule, your schedule will control you.

Jesus is a great example of living a full life but not a hurried life. He had plenty to do but was never rushed, and when others tried to push Him to go faster, He didn't. The gospel authors never say, "Jesus ran to help Mary," or "Jesus rushed to save the day." Yet we rush and hurry, basically living our lives running from one activity to the next. Does this take a toll on us? Absolutely. Living a hurried life drains us emotionally, physically, and spiritually. We ignore our wounds because ignoring them is quicker and easier than working through them. If you don't learn how to stop the hurry, you will keep running until you reach total exhaustion.

The good news is, you can learn to control your schedule, and you can learn to refuel. The solution is to add margin into your life. Margin is breathing room. Margin is a little reserve that you're not using up. You're not stretched to the limit in every area of your life.

When you build margin into your life, you will experience more peace of mind, better health, less stress, stronger relationships, and more availability for loving like Jesus because you say "yes" to the right things instead of everything.

The question is, how do you build healthy margins into your life so that you don't feel like you are running on empty all day, every day?

Learn to accept your limitations.

You've got to recognize you have limits and come to the place where you accept them. *"I have learned that everything has limits,"* wrote the psalmist in Psalm 119:96 (GNT). We are only human, we are not invincible. We need sleep, food, and emotional rest. We have physical limitations, emotional limitations, time limitations, and mental limitations. God gave us limitations for our own good, and He instituted the Sabbath so we would take a day of rest in order to unplug and refuel. You can't be friends with everyone, but you can have a few friends. You can't operate on three hours of sleep a night, but you can operate on seven or eight. Rather than fighting your limits, you need to accept them. Instead of trying to fight your limitations, build your rhythms around them.

Learn to be content.

People who have margin in their lives have learned to be content with who they are and what they have. Stop comparing your life to everyone else's life and your stuff with everyone else's stuff. Learn your rhythms. Until you do, you will always be driven to take on more. Stop that constant push to pack your day full of stuff. The Old Testament says, *"It is better to have only a little, with peace of mind, than be busy all the time,"* (Ecclesiastes 4:6, GNT). Ask yourself a very frank question: Will having more and doing more make me happier? If you are not happy with what you have today, you're not going to be happy with what you get tomorrow because today you're not happy with what you were striving for yesterday.

Learn to say "no" a lot more.

You may be addicted to the lifestyle of going faster and faster and how important it makes you feel. We have to learn it is okay to say "no" to the unimportant things so we can say "yes" to the right things. It's always easier to fill your schedule than it is to empty your schedule. There are times when we have to just say "no." Just because something is a good cause doesn't mean it's your cause.

Take control of your calendar.

I covered this in a previous chapter but still need to say, if you don't take control of your schedule, your schedule will overtake you. I am not a calendar freak, but I do plan my days. If you don't have a plan, you will get sidetracked and feel like you were really busy all day but didn't accomplish anything, leaving you feeling frustrated. Other people are always happy to fill your calendar for you, but quite honestly, God has the best plan for your life, not them. Put your overstuffed schedule on a diet and stick to it.

Create intentional down time.

You will be far more likely to commit to taking some time off if you schedule it. Schedule a night for yourself or with friends.

Plan a day to shop or read. Take a day off, a whole day off. And don't feel guilty for planning down time. We all need it.

Set boundaries.

Boundaries include choosing when you will check your e-mail, texts, social media, or work outside of the office. Do you always have to be available? Decide what you will and will not allow to clutter up your calendar. This can be tricky, but is necessary. If you don't set boundaries, nobody is going to set them for you. Boundaries will need to flex occasionally, but you need to create them and do the best you can to live within them.

Limit social media time.

If you spend only five minutes checking social media but check it ten times a day, that's 50 minutes of your day that is gone forever. If you spend a lot of your time surfing social networks, make a change and start investing it in better ways.

Build margin into your life every day. King Solomon writes that it is foolishness to work all the time. *"Only someone too stupid to find his way home would wear himself out with work."* (Ecclesiastes 10:15, GNT). You don't have to be busy every moment of every day. Life is a journey to be experienced, not a race to be won. The truth is, if we want to last in life, we need to add margin to our schedules. Remember, it's not how fast you live that's important, it's how well you live.

Apply It

Write down one scheduled event you could unschedule to build some margin into your life. If you can think of two or three, list them as well:

I am committed to removing _____from
my calendar this week.

I am going to cancel _____ this
week.

_____

_____

_____

Engage With Your Emotions

Previous chapters have spoken to this subject in great detail.
It's important to engage with your emotions because it is essential
to caring for your soul. When you lose touch with your emotions,
life feels numb. You need to learn how to process conflict, failure,
and success before they turn into wounds or pride.

Pastor Chris Hodges' book, *Fresh Air*, included a powerful
lesson for me. He wrote about the origins of the term "doldrum."
Long before diesel- or steam-powered vessels, sailing ships ruled
the seas. Sailors were completely dependent on the wind. When
the wind blew, they would hoist their sails to catch the wind.
Sailors didn't fear sharks or the wide open sea; they feared the
Doldrums. "The Doldrums" refers to those parts of the Atlantic
and Pacific Oceans affected by the Intertropical Convergence
Zone, a low-pressure area around the equator where the prevailing
winds are calm.[31] If a ship drifted off-course, or the Doldrums
slightly shifted, a ship would sail into a dead zone. It didn't
matter if they hoisted every sail, where there was no wind, there
was no movement. The ship would stop sailing and just float. A

---

31   "What Are the Doldrums?" NOAA's National Ocean Service. July 15,
2016. https://oceanservice.noaa.gov/facts/doldrums.html.

ship could get stuck in the Doldrums for days or even weeks. The sailors would get depressed because there was absolutely nothing they could do but wait until the winds blew again. Many sailing crews consumed their entire provisions waiting for the wind to blow. Some unfortunate souls eventually starved to death waiting for winds that never came.

The word doldrums is derived from *dold*, an archaic term meaning stupid, and *rum(s)*, a noun suffix found in such words as conundrum. Early sailors called this miserable area the Doldrums because when the winds stopped blowing, their spirits started sinking. People use the term today to describe feeling lethargic, mildly depressed, or stagnant. Everyone is going to sail into an emotional doldrum from time to time.

You will experience periods when you feel emotionally stagnant, lethargic, or mildly-depressed, just trying to survive long enough for a fresh wind to blow. Learn to decipher how you feel and why you feel that way. You can do that by describing your emotional state audibly or on paper. This will help you process your emotions in healthy ways.

Apply It

Answer the following questions to help you understand how you feel right now. This will help you to connect with your emotions.

My physical body is _____ (tired, rested, tense, etc.)

I am getting _____ (plenty of, some, little, too much) sleep.

I feel _____ (excited, bored, happy,

sad, lonely, isolated, recharged, drained, frustrated, angry, anxious, stressed-out, fragmented, overwhelmed, stretched, eager, blah, etc.)

I am having a _____ (hard, easy) time describing how I feel.

If you are having a hard time describing how you feel, go back to question three and read each word intentionally. What words stand out to you? They may portray your true feelings.

It can be very hard to get in touch with your emotions if you have spent most of your life disconnected from them.

Care for Your Physical Body

I can't emphasize enough how important it is to take care of your body. Our dietary patterns, sleep habits, and exercise routines (or lack thereof) are all important aspects of soul care. When I was in my late teens and twenties, my body just seemed to work. I didn't work out, eat healthy, or get enough rest. In spite of my poor health habits, I didn't have any significant physical problems. Then I turned thirty. I gained a few pounds and started feeling the effects of lack of exercise, a poor diet, stress, and minimal sleep.

As the years continue to roll on, caring for your physical body becomes more and more important. Your body isn't like a fine wine that gets better with age; your body is more like a car that needs regular maintenance to keep it running smoothly. The more miles a car has on it, the more maintenance it typically needs.

Exercise.

I am not a health nut, but the statistical reality is that exercise adds vitality and energy to your life. Exercise will increase your energy level. Several years ago, I started working out. I do it because I need the energy. I get sick less, and it helps lower my stress. I started exercising after one of my mentor pastors said if I wanted to last in ministry I needed to take care of myself physically. He was right. I walk on the treadmill for a while, then lift a few weights. It is a simple routine that has helped me stay relatively fit. I'm trying to avoid that unique pear shape I get when I put on too many extra pounds. The apostle John wrote, *"Dear friend, I pray that you may enjoy good health and that all may go well with you, even as your soul is getting along well,"* (3 John 1:2). Paul says something similar in 1 Corinthians 6:19–20. I feel better physically and mentally after exercising and you will, too.

If you are tired of being tired, it's time to do something about it. Don't start by planning to exercise for an hour a day. You will just set yourself up for failure. But you can start by walking up the stairs at the office or parking your car in the back of the lot at the store so you need to walk farther. Take a stroll around the block or up and down the road. If you have a dog, it will be elated with your new routine.

Get proper rest.

The quality of your sleep directly affects your mental and physical health. If you get good solid rest, the quality of your waking life will improve. Your productivity will go up, you will have better mental focus and clarity, and your immune system will be healthier, improving your ability to fight illness. No other activity gives you so many benefits with so little effort.

There will be times when you won't be able to rest as much as you need, but this should be the exception and not the rule. Adjust your schedule to accommodate adequate rest. The amount of sleep a person needs varies slightly depending on age. Most healthy adults between the ages of twenty-six and sixty-four need from seven to nine hours of sleep per night to function at their best. Children and teens require more sleep than adults because their bodies are still developing (nine to eleven hours of sleep). The notion that people don't need as much sleep when they get older is false. People over sixty-five still need at least seven hours of sleep to function at their best. Older adults who have trouble sleeping at night can take naps during the day.[32]

Eat right.

My wife, Kathi, has a 45-minute commute to work each day. She is in good health and looks great. This past year she noticed her ankles would be swollen at the end of the day, and her toes were like little sausages. Even though she got plenty of sleep, she was tired often. Then she decided to change her diet. She started eating healthy food and stopped eating sugar. Within nine months she had lost close to twenty pounds. She had more energy, needed less sleep, started getting up earlier in the morning, and noticed the swelling in her feet had gone away. That's not all. Her joints ached less, she had better mental clarity, and overall she just felt better. Changing her diet made a significant impact on Kathi's overall quality of life.

32   Smith, Melinda, Lawrence Robinson, and Robert Segal. "Sleep Needs." HelpGuide.org. March 21, 2019. Accessed January 11, 2019. https://www. helpguide.org/articles/sleep/sleep-needs-get-the-sleep-you-need.htm/.

Eating right is important for your physical body. A proper diet is just as important as rest and exercise. You don't have to eat cabbage and drink vegetable juice at every meal, but you do need to develop and maintain healthy eating habits. Eat nutritious meals in reasonable quantities. Cut down on the sugar and processed foods. A proper diet will help you to feel more energized and give you better mental clarity.

Apply It

This week how will you care for your physical body?

This week my sleep goal is _____ hours per night.

This week I will exercise on these days:

_____ I will exercise for this amount of time each day: _____ .

This week I will be conscious of what I eat and how much I eat. I will start to make changes to my diet, starting with this: _____ .

Prioritize life-giving relationships

Significant, life-giving relationships are essential to a healthy life. Relationships help restore your emotional energy, thus filling your soul. Invest your time developing a few good friends instead of trying to be friends with everyone. Jesus had three close male friends—John, Peter, and James. He was also close friends with Mary, Martha, and Lazarus. These were His "refrigerator friends." A refrigerator friend is someone you are so close to that you can dig around in each other's refrigerators without thinking twice. They know where you keep the butter and that secret chocolate bar.

Life-giving relationships should start with your immediate family. Your family relationships should be refreshing. When I am with my family, I feel connected and filled. We don't always have to go somewhere or do something together; just being around them fills my relational bucket. Sometimes they still annoy me, but that's just life. It is important for you to carve out time for your family, no matter what your family situation looks like.

Not every family relationship is healthy. Family systems are complex and difficult to keep intact. They take work and effort to maintain and strengthen. You might have to ask for forgiveness or put in some extra effort to get things back on track. I don't know your situation, but I do know you need to do your best to have life-giving relationships with your family.

I used to dread hauling my kids around from event to event and activity to activity. I was always in the car, picking up one of them from hockey, choir, or some other after-school activity. I spent hours and hours just driving to and from events every week. After doing this for years, my attitude started to go south. I was crabby around the kids, angry I had to stop what I was doing so I could drive them. It felt like a waste of my time.

That all changed when I decided to take advantage of the time I had with them to build our relationships. Now, I use our time together to talk or listen to them, depending on what's going on in their lives. Sometimes they have a lot to say, and other times they want to sit and play on their phones. Several years ago, I decided that when I am with them in the car, I will do my best to not be on the phone. And for the most part, I'm not. Every once in a while, I need to take a call, but I usually ask them first or tell the caller I will get back to them. I want to send my kids the message they are important to me, and I do that by prioritizing them, even when they want to play on their phones. Now instead of dreading our daily drives, I actually cherish them.

I also prioritize life-giving friendships. My refrigerator friends are important to me because they fill me. I have a lot of acquaintances and very few close friends. I'm okay with that. Acquaintances say, "Hi" and friends say, "How are you?" because they care. Friends take the time to enjoy a second cup of coffee with you.

People are like Legos; they only have so many pegs to connect with. If you want to be friends with someone who doesn't have any more relational pegs left to connect with, look for someone who does have some pegs left. This can be difficult, but keep trying. My life-giving relationships are important to me, so I make time for them. You should, too.

Apply It

Am I spending enough time with my immediate family?

_____

What do I need to change in order to spend more time with them? _____

Write down the names of up to three of your good friends. What do you enjoy about these relationships? (Describe in writing.)

_____

_____

_____

_____

_____

Do you schedule regular times to meet with your close friends? When are you going to get together again?

Manage your finances well

I spent years living from paycheck to paycheck and working two jobs. To save money, I learned how to fix and repair anything and everything. Kathi and I drove old cars with thousands of miles on them, they needed constant repairs. No matter how hard I worked, we were still strapped, and I felt the pressure. We spent years being broke and struggling just to survive.

When you are financially strapped, it takes a serious toll on your soul. It impacts every area of life—your sleep, your physical health, and your mental wellbeing. Some people are financially stretched because they don't know how to manage the money they have. Others are broke because they simply don't make enough money to pay for even simple necessities.

I am convinced that it is possible to achieve financial contentment and financial freedom but it takes work, discipline, and commitment. You can take steps to manage your finances well, and doing so will increase your quality of life. Being faithful with finances leads to contentment. Six principles have helped turn my financial situation around. And, while they haven't made me rich, I am not poor either. My soul has found financial peace by being content with what I have.

1. Commit to trusting God with all of your finances, not just the leftovers. We trust God with our health, our families, our problems, and so many other things, but when it comes to our finances, we say, "Wait a minute, I know how to handle my money better than God." Then we apply our own principles and end up going backward.

The Bible talks about money more than love, grace, and forgiveness. Why does God have so much to say about how we handle money? Because He knew we would be pretty bad at it. God gives you financial principles because He loves you and wants you to prosper, not suffer. God promises He will provide for your needs. One of the very names of God is *Jehovah-jireh*, which is Hebrew for "the Lord will provide," (Genesis 22:14). God's nature doesn't change. The apostle Paul wrote, "*My God will meet all your needs according to his glorious riches in Christ Jesus*," (Philippians 4:19). I believe this to be true and have experienced it myself.

God is predictable in His faithfulness to provide for your needs. He *will* provide for your needs, that is His promise. But, there is a degree of unpredictability in how God provides. God fed the Israelites wandering in the desert for forty years with manna every morning and quail every night. Moses never saw that one coming and neither did anyone else. He fed Elijah by a raven and hydrated him with a brook. You could have given Elijah a thousand guesses about how God would provide for him, and I bet he never would have thought a raven would be bringing him his food. The same God who fed five thousand with only five loaves and two fish has promised to provide for your needs too, so trust him completely. How he does it may surprise you.

2. Commit to applying God's financial principles to your life today. The Bible is full of financial principles that will help you have a better life if you live by them. Why does God suggest that you live debt-free? Because without debt you experience less stress, have more financial freedom, and are able to give generously. Why does God suggest that you pay your bills? Because if you don't, you may face legal consequences. There could also be relational stress and tension. If you don't pay your bills, you are essentially stealing goods and services. Why does God suggest you tithe (giving the first ten percent of your income back to God)? Because He owns everything anyway, and when you tithe, He promises to bless you for it. Tithing is one tangible way you can say thank you to God and be a part of His church around the world.

3. **Take a financial inventory of how you spend your money right now.** Have you ever thought how much money you spend on coffee per week? Media? Going out to eat? Most people spend far more everyday on stuff they don't need than they would ever admit. As you assess what you spend your money on, cut out what you don't need so you are spending less. This may mean going out to eat once or twice a month instead of ten times a month. It might mean you shop around for a new phone plan. Learn to buy used when you can, think thrifty, use coupons, and be a good steward of what you have. Your money will go much further than you think.

4. **Cut back on your spending.** This isn't rocket science, but it does take discipline. Stop chasing after things and stuff and experiences you can't afford. If you have the money, spend it and enjoy it. But if you don't have the money, don't go into debt. Live within your means. The Bible says, "Indulging in luxuries, wine, and food will never make you wealthy," (Proverbs 21:17, GNT).

I learned this the hard way. When I was twenty and serving in the Air Force, I bought a brand new car that I thought I could afford. Turns out, I couldn't afford it. For six months, I ate hot dogs and noodles, that I cooked in my coffee pot, because I was too poor to buy decent food. I was spending all my money on car payments and auto insurance. My loving father took over my car payments when I was sent to Germany, and that's the only way I got out of debt. Now that I am older, I get it; I now know just how important it is to spend within my means. The only way to do that is to have some type of budget. We will talk about that later.

People tend to think that the more money they spend on an experience or item, the more it will be appreciated. That is not always true. Some of the best experiences you have had cost you very little money. Think back to your childhood. What are some of your best memories? Do they involve a vacation or playing in the yard? Who was there and what did you do? Chances are your best memory didn't cost your parents a fortune. Your best memory probably wasn't that trip to Disney World that cost your parents ten grand. Your best memory probably has more to do with who you were with and what you did than the cost of the activity itself.

Once, a friend gave me five three-day passes to Disney World. The kids were all old enough to enjoy it and be somewhat self-sufficient, so it was the best time to go. It cost us a ton to fly to Florida and rent a car. Kathi got us a sweet deal on a hotel, but it still cost a fortune. I had fantasies of my kids telling me how much they loved me as they experienced It's a Small World and some of the other amazing rides. Instead, our trip was awful. The crowds were huge, and my family doesn't do well with crowds. The food cost a fortune, and I don't like spending so much money on food. One day it rained. Josh, Kathi, and Katie didn't like rides; Sara did. On our second day there, I took the kids to three parks; they were so tired they didn't even enjoy it.

After the Disney fiasco, we drove to a friend's house, where we spent the next few days. We didn't go anywhere or do anything except go to the beach, swim, and eat. We played games and watched movies at night; the kids loved it. My kids had the most fun at the beach and just hanging out, which was free. Looking back, most of the best memories I have with my family don't include spending a ton of money. It was the simple times when we were together that have left the best memories.

5. **Save up an emergency fund.** Do this by saving a thousand dollars and putting it in an emergency fund. It might take a while to do, but once you have it and something breaks, you won't go into a panic or overextend yourself with credit cards to fix it.

Money will always be a part of your life. If you manage it wisely, it can bring you a lot of joy and pleasure, and bring glory to God. If you mismanage it and overspend, you will feel the weight of debt, and it will hurt. Once the love of money grabs your heart and fills it with unquenchable desires, you will become a slave to money, and it will cause wounds instead of benefits.

Apply It

Do you have a budget? Do you stick to it? If not, commit yourself to starting one. You should be able to find a good budget worksheet online.

Enjoy ample recreation

The early believers enjoyed spending time together. It helped them feel connected and encouraged. Luke wrote, *"Every day they continued to meet together in the temple courts. They broke bread in their homes and ate together with glad and sincere hearts,"* (Acts 2:46). Meeting together was a type of recreation for them.

What fills you up? Do you like to watch movies or bike or try different restaurants or hang out with friends? Find something to do that fills your bucket and put it in your schedule. I used to feel guilty for taking a day off from work. There was so much to do and so many needs to be met that I had wrongly convinced myself taking time off was neglecting my responsibilities. I still work long, hard hours, but I also know I need to take time off to enjoy activities that replenish me. I love to ride my motorcycle in the summer and snowmobile in the winter. I enjoy fishing and tinkering around the house. I also enjoy playing hockey and polishing rocks. I know when I work too much because I abandon all my hobbies and life loses its color. When I am depleted life turns gray.

Apply It

Write down five recreational activities that you enjoy. This will help you to reflect on the things that help you feel content. What recreational activities breathe wind into your sails? Here are a few examples that might resonate with you:

- Watching sports
- Playing sports
- Fishing
- Hunting
- Horseback riding
- Motorcycling
- Skiing
- Taking walks
- Running
- Eating out with friends
- Going to see a movie
- Playing video games
- Reading
- Working on a car
- Woodworking

What five recreational activities fill your tank?

_____

_____

_____

_____

_____

Fill your spirit

Filling your spirit involves intentionally connecting with God in meaningful ways every day. When I'm connected to God, the rest of my life feels manageable. When I feel God's love and open to the Holy Spirit's gentle promptings, my quality of life goes up.

Psalm 23 is one of the most recognized passages of Scripture. We read it anytime we need God to comfort us. But if you back up one chapter to Psalm 22, you see a completely different picture. We don't read this psalm for comfort,

My God, my God, why have you forsaken me? Why are you so far from saving me, so far from my cries of anguish? My God, I cry out by day, but you do not answer, by night, but I find no rest. (Psalm 22:1–2)

These verses speak prophetically of Christ on the cross, but on another level, they also echo our human frustrations. Have you ever shouted, "God, my life is out of control! I'm in anguish! Where are You? I'm exhausted!"? I have.

Psalm 23 paints a completely different picture. Psalm 23 was written by David who was completely dependent on God.

The Lord is my shepherd, I lack nothing. He makes me lie down in green pastures, he leads me beside quiet waters, he refreshes my soul. He guides me along the right

paths for his name's sake. Even though I walk through the darkest valley, I will fear no evil, for you are with me; your rod and your staff, they comfort me. (Psalm 23:1–4)

Psalm 23 declares that if you trust God for everything, you won't lack anything. When you are connected to Christ, it is easier to trust Him in all things. David continues in verses two and three to say God leads him to green pastures. This is a metaphor for a good place to be. You want to be led to green pastures, and you want to be led to a great place. But in order for that to happen, you need to be connected to God so you can sense where He is leading you.

Verse four has brought comfort to many people who are knocking on death's door. But it can also be applied to the living. Do you feel so overwhelmed that you are dying on the inside? This verse is about trusting God and letting Him guide you and lead you through life. Be content with who He made you to be. You don't have to do more to be worth more. You are already valuable.

What's interesting is, as more and more people came to Jesus to have their needs met, He needed more time alone with God. He had to retreat to recharge. Luke 5:15–16 records,

"Yet the news about him spread all the more, so that crowds of people came to hear him and to be healed of their sicknesses. But Jesus often withdrew to lonely places and prayed."

Why did Jesus retreat? He needed to connect with His heavenly Father. This filled His spiritual tank; He was able to recharge. Since Jesus came in the flesh, He had to accept His physical limitations and learn how to recharge.

One time, I was meeting with a good friend and mentor,

describing how empty and numb I felt. He asked me if I practiced pausing. I must have looked at him funny because he went on to explain what pausing is. Pausing involves sitting still for a few minutes just being present in the moment. You take a slow deep breath in then exhale, letting your whole body relax. Put your hands on your lap and don't move around. Just pause and be fully present in the moment. Listen to the sounds around you, stare at the sky, do whatever you want, as long as you remain still.

I designated one chair in my house as my pausing chair. I will sit in it and just stare out the window for a few minutes. While I sit there, I open my heart to God. I'm not good at slowing down, so at first, this was really hard. I could sit for about thirty seconds before checking my phone or fiddling with something. But now, several times a week, I will sit in my chair and be open to God. Sometimes I pray for my family or other people. Sometimes I reflect on my goals and ask God to help me focus on what's important. To be fully present in the moment, I like to pause just before or just after reading the Bible. Sometimes God puts someone's name on my heart, and I write it down and phone them later. Essentially, I pause so I can connect with God, which replenishes me and fills my spirit. You can do this too. Pick a place and set a time. Put it on your calendar if you need to.

Apply It

What spiritual activities lift you up, helping you connect with Christ? Write three of them down. For example:

- Reading the Bible
- Listening to a podcast
- Attending church
- Serving others

- Prayer
- Singing worship music
- Listening to worship music
- Participating in a Bible study
- Talking about theology with a close friend
- Spending time outdoors
- Sitting in silence

Practice a "pause." Find a quiet place and focus on your breathing and being present in the moment for just five minutes. At first, it will seem like an eternity, but after you pause a few times, it will refresh your soul.

Check your gauges

Each soul care area is like a gauge that you can check by asking reflective questions. How you answer each question reveals the condition of your soul in that particular area.

- Do I have margin in my life?
- Am I in touch with my emotions?
- Am I caring for my physical body?
- Am I prioritizing life-giving relationships?
- Am I managing my finances well?
- Am I spending adequate time in recreation?
- Do I feel spiritually filled?

If you have margin in your life, is an indicator that you have a healthy schedule. If you are in touch with your emotions, that is an indicator that you are emotionally healthy or know the work you need to do. If you are overcommitted, that is an indicator that your soul is being drained. If you feel numb, that is an indicator your emotional tank is low and you need to get in touch with your emotions. Your soul gauges will move based on your life circumstances. If you are not paying attention to them, it could cause significant damage.

Apply It

On a scale of 1 to 10 how full is your soul tank? Be honest in your rating. (It may even be riding on "empty.")

Write down five things that drain your soul. These things can be tasks, interpersonal matters, or social endeavors. The goal is to bring to the surface all of the life-draining, soul-sucking stuff cluttering up your life. Here are a few examples of things that drain me:

- Pointless meetings
- Challenging family relationships
- Paying bills
- Cleaning the kitchen
- Reading e-mails messages others have told me are important but are not
- Bad relationships
- Trying to keep up on social media
- Volunteering for the wrong things
- Having every waking hour of every day scheduled out
- Being on too many task forces, teams, or committees
- Cleaning up after my kids
- Listening to people whine on and on
- Loading the water softener with salt

If you can't pinpoint what sucks the life out of you, ask a "refrigerator friend" to help. Sometimes others know what drains you more than you do because they see the physical and emotional changes reflected in your countenance or demeanor.

Now that you have identified what drains your soul, it's time to think about what it feels like when your soul is healthy. What does it feel like when you feel emotionally healthy, spiritually healthy, physically healthy, financially healthy, relationally healthy, recreationally healthy, and have margin in your life? Do you remember? Write down how you feel when your tank is full. For example, when my tank is full...

- I feel happy.
- I feel like spending time with friends.
- I feel more productive.
- I feel like I make better choices.
- I am less agitated.
- I am more caring and compassionate.
- I am more creative.
- I am more giving.
- I am more loving.
- I am less stressed.

I want to lovingly reassure you that you can change your situation, and when you do, your soul tank will be filled. It's not hopeless; God has not given up on you. On more than one occasion, I have looked at my own gauges and realized I needed to make changes. As your life changes, you will have to make changes, too. If you want to care for your soul it's going to take a concerted effort and willingness to make moving adjustments along the way. You will need to be honest with yourself and pray for the courage and willingness to persevere. I can tell you from personal experience that when you care for your soul, you will reap incredible rewards. Rewards such as:

- More satisfaction
- More contentment
- More peace
- Less hurry

- More productivity
- More feelings of engagement
- More spiritual strength
- More emotional stability

God is willing to fill your soul tank if you let Him. Give Him access to your heart and be willing to make the changes you know you need to make. Your life can get better, and you can start to feel whole again.

Pick one thing right now that drains you and stop doing it, if at all possible. You can't drop everything, but there is at least one thing you can just let go of. Is it going to the gym every day? Having a perfect lawn? What one thing can you let go of? Write it down: "This week I am letting go of _____."

Now, write one thing that you can do this week to refuel your soul tank. Do you want to spend more time with a friend? Read a book? Take a walk? Think of something you can do that is tangible and will reap immediate benefits. Write it down: "This week I am going to do this: _____.

You can care for your own soul. It all starts with a commitment to follow the principles outlined in this chapter. Start today, and each week revisit your schedule to make necessary adjustments. Let go of the things you need to let go of so that you can whatever you want to do more of or prioritize. These intentional decisions will start to set your life back in rhythm providing you with a sense of fulfillment and accomplishment. One decision at a time, you will move from wounded to wonderful.

CHAPTER 9

STAYING HEALTHY

The *Bourne Identity* movies are probably my favorite action films of all time. I know it's just a movie, but Jason Bourne is one of the toughest people ever. If you have no idea what I'm talking about, you have missed some of the greatest movies ever.

The movie begins with an unconscious man floating in the Mediterranean Sea. He is spotted and subsequently plucked from his watery grave by a group of Italian fishermen. The ship's captain removes two slugs from the mystery man's back when something suspicious on the man's hip catches his eye. Moments later, he removes a small, strange capsule containing a Swiss bank account number. As the mystery man starts to physically heal, his memory does not. The only clue as to who he is was found in that strange, capsule leading him to a safe-deposit box in Zurich, Switzerland. He travels to Switzerland, rummages through the contents of the safety-deposit box, and discovers that his name is Jason Bourne. From there, he expects to learn more about who he is after a visit to the American consulate. Instead of discovering his identity, Bourne suddenly finds himself on the run from his own government. Someone wants Jason Bourne dead, and fast. But Bourne is elusive. He can fight like a ninja, speak multiple languages, and stay one step ahead of his enemies no matter where he is. Bourne eventually learns he has a storied past. He is actually a black-ops assassin for a clandestine Central Intelligence Agency who has outlived his usefulness. In the end, Jason Bourne discovers his real name is David Webb, but he still can't remember who he is.

Have you ever stared into the depths of your own eyes reflected back at you in a mirror? Have you ever asked yourself, "Who am I?" I had a vivid imagination as a child. Sometimes I would lie in bed, staring at the ceiling, wondering if my parents were aliens cleverly disguised as people. I would scrutinize them, trying to figure out if they were wearing human costumes. On several occasions, I wondered if they had a secret space ship buried beneath the house. It sounds silly, but my doubts were birthed in a pool of insecurity. I was adopted when I was nine months old and have never met my biological parents. As a child, I often wondered who my biological parents were. What did they look like? What did they do for a living? Did I have any brothers or sisters? Were they rich and influential? All these questions were like missing pieces in my puzzle, and no matter how hard I tried, I just could not see the complete picture of me. I have never sought out my birth parents and am not sure if I ever will. To be honest, it would provide some answers, but for now I am content just being a child of God and the adopted son of two amazing parents named Ross and Char—who are not aliens at all.

Where do you find your identity? If only everyone could find their own unique identity and be happy with who they are, but that simply isn't true. People find their identity in many places. Men and women often use their jobs, relationships, physical attributes, heritage, and material possessions to define themselves. Over time, these descriptors can define you. For example, if you anchor your identity to your occupation, what happens when your occupation changes? Anchoring your identity to your occupation is risky. If you lose your job, you will become like Jason Bourne. If you tie your personal worth to your net worth, what happens if you have financial trouble? Your bank account should never define you.

Identity in Accomplishments

Some people define who they are by what they have done, but that doesn't work either. There is nothing wrong with accomplishment—I am all for it. But you are not the sum total of what you have done. If you think this way and fail to meet a deadline or reach your goal, you won't only be upset because you didn't reach your goal, but you risk labeling yourself as a failure. People who fail to meet their own expectations tend to stand in front of the mirror and hurl insults at themselves for not measuring up.

Identity in Public Opinion

Your identity is not derived from other people's opinions of you. Opinions are like belly buttons. Everybody has one, and no two are the same. You will go crazy if you try to be the person that others think favorably of. If someone doesn't like one of your posts on social media or something you do, it won't only hurt you emotionally; it will rock your identity. People who play to the crowd will make compromises to win the crowd's approval at any cost. This creates an incredible amount of internal dissatisfaction because there will always be someone else to impress and a storefront image to maintain.

Identity in Your Body

Your identity is not found in your body image. If you try to find your identity in your body image, you will be fiercely devoted to your outward appearance. People obsessed with their appearance spend copious sums of money toning, trimming, and sculpting their bodies. One's body image can actually become an idol. Others who are engrossed in their body image will self-bash and never feel content in their own skin.

Identity From Relationships

Your identity is not based on your relationships. While it is important to have and enjoy life-giving relationships, you should never look for your identity in them. Trying to find your identity in relationships doesn't work. People may move, and they will disappoint you or let you down. Your feelings may change. When that happens, you will feel like you have lost your identity, so you start hunting for someone else to make you feel complete. A big portion of your wounds came from other people, so why try to find your identity in them?

Where do you find your real identity?

Elijah McCoy was born in 1844 in Ontario, Canada to George and Mildred, both runaway slaves from Kentucky who escaped on the underground railway. When he was three, his parents returned to the United States and settled in Detroit, Michigan.

Elijah was fascinated by machinery in his youth and decided to turn his passion into a lifelong career by becoming an engineer.

While working as a fireman on the Michigan Central Railroad, Elijah invented an automatic lubricator for oiling the steam engines of locomotives, boats, and other motorized transportation. He received his first patent on July 12, 1872. Elijah McCoy's invention revolutionized the railroad industry because it allowed trains to run longer and more reliably, thus saving the railroad thousands in maintenance costs.

Elijah also invented several other very useful products we still use today. He patented the first folding ironing board and a lawn sprinkler. His inventions were so good that hundreds of other companies tried to copy his products. His automatic lubricator for locomotives was so good that all the maintenance hands who worked on the trains always knew when they were working with a cheap imitation or "the Real McCoy."[33]

In a spiritual sense, the Real McCoy is Jesus Christ. You need to accept and embrace who you are in Christ. That is where you will find your true identity because you are God's creation, His masterpiece. You can anchor your life on this truth. The psalmist wrote, *"Thank you for making me so wonderfully complex! Your workmanship is marvelous—how well I know it,"* (Psalm 139:14, NLT).

If you try to find your identity in anything other than Christ,

---

33   Martin Rywell (chief compiler), Charles H. Wesley, et al., *Afro-American Encyclopedia*, vol. VI (North Miami, Fla.: Educational Book Publishers, 1974), 617. Harry A. Ploski, Ernest Kaiser, *Afro USA: A Reference Work on the Black Experience* (New York: Bellwether Publishing Co., 1971), 732. James C. Williams (compiler), *At Last Recognition in America: A Reference Handbook of Unknown Black Inventors and their Contribution to America*, vol. 1 (Chicago: BCA Publishing Co., 1978), 31–32. *Dictionary of American Biography*, Vol. 11, Part 1 (New York: Scribner's, 1964), 617.

you are settling for a cheap imitation that will eventually fail, fall, or crumble. Jesus was able to face the incredible demands of His mission—rejecting vicious verbal assaults and physical demands—because He knew exactly who He was. As a believer in Christ your life is anchored in Him and all of His promises. Because your life is anchored in Christ, you are a new creation.

Bad Labels

We have a tendency to label each other. Such labels can be a help or a hindrance. You might have kids, but you are not just "a mother" or "a father." You might have a felony on your record, but you are not just "a felon." You might have ADHD, as I do, but your condition doesn't define you. Your past doesn't define you. Your situation doesn't define you, nor do your failures or finances. You are a new creation in Christ. The apostle Paul got to the heart of this truth when he wrote, *"Therefore, if anyone is in Christ, he is a new creation. The old has passed away; behold, the new has come,"* (2 Corinthians 5:17, ESV).

Paul had a sketchy past, but his past didn't define him. Your past doesn't define you either. Anchor your life in Christ because you are a child of the King. If you mess up, confess up. Ask God to forgive you and move on. When someone labels you, either negatively or positively, don't let it define you. Stop accepting the labels others slap on you and reject the past labels you have given yourself. You're not defined by the bully you have created in your head. You're not defined by the opinions of others, social media comments, or by your circumstances. You're not defined by your successes or failures. Don't let your wounds define you. Abandon any image of yourself that is not from God. You are defined by God and God alone. He identifies you as His own. You are who

God says you are, and no one else has a vote in the matter.

In 1970, one of the greatest cars ever built rolled off the assembly line. The 1970 Chevy Chevelle was all muscle and all the rage. You could order it with a whole assortment of options from a 4-door with a V-6 engine to the head-turning power-packed Big Block 454. It came in a wide range of colors, from a dull green to a lustrous red. Although I was only one year old when the 1970 Chevelle came out, by the time I turned sixteen, I wanted one because to me it was the ultimate, must-have muscle car.

While in college, I was thumbing through the ads in the paper when I came across an ad for a 1970 Chevelle. The owner only wanted $700 for it, so I called him and drove straight to Minneapolis to look at it. I remember pulling up to the owner's house and seeing the car for the first time. It had bald tires, an orange hood, a dull red trunk, and didn't run. The rear quarter panels were rusty, and so were the front ones. With all that rust, it was definitely a Minnesota car. The seats were torn, and the carpet was in shambles. When the car had rolled off the assembly line in 1970, it was in great running condition, but years of use, abuse, Minnesota winters, and a few collisions had taken their toll. What once was a shiny new car was now just a clunker. The decision was easy for me. I coughed up $700, signed the title, and hooked up a tow bar to drag it home.

I remember showing it to my then girlfriend, now wife. I think Kathi supported my decision to buy it only because we were courting at the time. For the next year, all I could afford to do was look at it and take off the stuff I knew I didn't need. I eventually found front fenders, a hood, doors, and a bumper, so I bought them for $200 and put them on the car. The new parts were green; the old ones were orange and red. The car looked like it belonged in a circus more than in a parking lot. Shortly thereafter, Kathi and I got married, and the car was mothballed for a couple of years. We bought a house, and once again, project Chevelle was tabled. Over the next few years, I started removing damaged and rusty parts and bolting on new ones when I could afford them. I installed new rear axles, quarter panels, disc brakes, and power steering. Delete these sentences and replace with "For three years, I begged a friend to sell me a Big Block 454 engine to replace the non-functioning one. Once in my possession, another friend and I rebuilt and installed it.

At the time the car still didn't look like much, but I could envision what the car was becoming. It still was a patched-together piece of junk, but now it had a host of fancy SS parts on it. Piece by piece, I was turning the clunker into a classic. It took me five years to restore that car, and I enjoyed it for over 20 years. I finally sold it to buy a Mustang GT convertible.

When you and I came out of the "factory," we were in mint condition. But after years of long winters, door dings, crashes, and collisions, it's easy to feel rusted out, dented, and damaged. The good news is that God restores you and makes you a new creation in Christ.

In their book, *Your Whole Life*, Carol Showalter and Maggie Davis note that when a new highway is built,

> Workers have to clear land, cut down trees, dig up stumps, and truck in lots of new materials. Many roads are created through solid rock or deep woods. To create new habit patterns one needs to work as hard to construct a new road in the brain as it takes construction workers to build a new highway. We work, work and work, and

many times it just doesn't look like there will ever be a new highway. Then one day you realize you are on a new road.[34]

When I first brought that 1970 Chevelle home, people said it was a piece of junk and it was going to take way too much work to restore. Person after person looked at it and only saw a hulk that was in severe disrepair. But me, I saw the potential it had. Every time I closed my eyes, I pictured a shiny red Chevelle with a smooth-running 454. Even before the thing ran, I could feel the shifter in my hand as I slammed my foot to the ground. I saw the potential while others could only see the present. In order to live as a new creation in Christ, you need to believe the truth that you are a new creation in Christ. You need to believe God can heal your wounds and restore you. God sees your potential even if all you can see are your problems. As a child of God, you can claim your new identity in Christ; the old has gone, and the new has come.

Be Complete in Christ

Being a new creation in Christ means you are complete. You don't have to be married to be complete; you don't have to have kids to be complete. You don't need financial security, or a great job, or the ability to speak three languages. You don't need to own a nice car or house, and you don't have to have a zillion Facebook friends to be complete. Jesus completes you. The apostle Paul eloquently explains, *"So you also are complete through your union with Christ, who is the head over every ruler and authority,"* (Colossians 2:10, NLT).

Being complete in Christ means:

1. You are a new creation. (2 Corinthians 5:17)

---

34   Carol Showalter and Maggie Davis, Your Whole Life (Brewster, Mass.: Paraclete Press, 2010), 136.

2. You are justified. (Romans 5:1)

3. You are God's workmanship. (Ephesians 2:10)

4. You are free forever from condemnation.
   (Romans 8:1–2)

5. You are assured that all things work together for your
   good. (Romans 8:28)

6. You are able to do all things through Christ who
   strengthens you. (Philippians 4:13)

7. You are a member of Christ's body.
   (1 Corinthians 12:27)

8. You are adopted as God's child. (Ephesians 1:5)

9. You are the salt and light of the earth.
   (Matthew 5:13–14)

10. You are redeemed and forgiven. (Colossians 1:14)

11. You are able to find grace and mercy. (Hebrews 4:16)

12. You are confident that the good work God has
    begun in you will be perfected. (Philippians 1:6)

13. You are Christ's friend. (John 15:15)

14. You have not been given a spirit of fear, but of
    power, love and a sound mind. (2 Timothy 1:7)

15. You cannot be separated from the love of God.
    (Romans 8:38–39)[35]

If you try to find your identity in anything other than Christ,
you will come up empty-handed. People, things, accomplish-

---

35   Modified from "Who You Are in Christ," (http://biblestudyplanet.com/
who-you-are-in-christ), accessed July 3, 2018.

ments—all of it other than Christ—leads down a dead-end road that you can avoid, so avoid it. Find your identity in Christ.

Give Yourself a Check-Up

For years I have driven cars that have exceeded their life expectancy. Once I bought a minivan straight out of the junkyard. It ran, but not well. I limped it home, then gave it a full inspection. The van needed new spark plugs, spark plug wires, tires, an oil change, and many other parts just to make it roadworthy. After replacing the old, worn-out parts with new and used ones, the van was ready to hit the open road again. It quickly became one of my favorite vehicles even though it was a minivan. (Don't judge me!) After I repaired it, the van was very reliable, providing my family with transportation.

Every month, I would check the oil and other fluids. I rotated the tires and replaced the brakes when they became worn. With a little maintenance and regular inspections to make sure everything worked as it should, the van never left me stranded.

In the same way, you need to inspect your life on a regular basis to see if there are areas in need of work or repair. If your calendar is overloaded, a quick inspection will help you to take corrective action. If your physical body is ailing, give yourself a check-up—go see the doctor if you need to, change your diet, get regular exercise and plenty of rest. Take an emotional inventory to see if you need to forgive someone, work through a frustration, or reconnect with God. Since you are in control of your life, you are also responsible to maintain it. Maintenance is an important part of soul care and will enable you to stay healthy.

Stay Focused

The *Titanic* was a British passenger liner that sank in the North Atlantic Ocean in the early morning of April 15, 1912, after colliding with an iceberg during her maiden voyage from Great Britain to the United States. The *Titanic* was the largest ship afloat at the time it entered service, and people said it was unsinkable. Many of the wealthiest and influential people in the world were aboard the ship when it left Europe for America.

One of my coworkers and I took the time to tour the *Titanic* exhibit while we were at a recent conference. We had the chance to see many objects recovered from the ship including, plates and glassware, perfume, clothing, soap dishes, and other hardware. One of the exhibits included a metal piece of the ship itself that was torn from the side as it sank. I was able to touch it, and even though it was just a piece of metal, it was a stark reminder of a terrible tragedy that could have been avoided. I was impressed with all the artifacts I saw, but one artifact stood out more than all the rest. It was a pair of binoculars. The reason they stood out to me is because these binoculars could have prevented the *Titanic* from sinking.

Captain Edward Smith knew the *Titanic* was traveling through iceberg-filled waters. He knew there was danger, but he trusted his ship and his crew to make the journey safely. Two crewmen were assigned to iceberg watch, and on that cold and calm night, they had to stand way up in the crow's nest and watch for icebergs. The water was calm that night, and the stars were shining brightly. They reflected off the water, making it very hard to tell where the sky ended and the water began. Since there were no waves, the men could not see if any water splashed off the side of an iceberg. They were also in a hurry to get to their post and forgot to grab the binoculars, which would have enabled them to see any danger well in advance so they could inform the captain to turn the ship.

So the two men sat in the crow's nest peering off into the distance, blind to the danger right in front of them because they didn't take the time to pick up the only tool that could have saved them. By the time they saw the iceberg dead ahead with their naked eyes, there was nothing they could do. On April 14, 1912, just four days into the crossing, the *Titanic* hit an iceberg at 11:40 p.m. ship's time. The collision caused the ship's hull plates to buckle inward along her starboard side and opened five of her sixteen watertight compartments to the sea, sealing her fate. The unsinkable ship was going down. The sinking resulted in the loss of more than 1,500 passengers and crew, out of the 2,224 on board, making it one of the deadliest commercial peacetime maritime disasters in modern history, all because one person failed to bring one pair of binoculars. The *Titanic* didn't have to sink; it wasn't destined for the bottom. It sank because two people simply forgot to bring the one thing that could have saved them all.

If you want to stay healthy you need to stay focused on Christ. He created you, loves you, sustains you, cares for you, and wants a deeper relationship with you. How many "life-bergs" could be avoided if you just focused on Him?

Persevere

There is no magic pill or prayer that will anchor your life to Christ; it is going to take grit. Dr. Angela Duckworth and her research team at the University of Pennsylvania give a profoundly useful definition of the word "grit." She explains that "true grit is perseverance and passion for long-term goals." Grit is courage, not just in the moment but sustained over time, in the ongoing pursuit of challenging objectives. People with grit are able to persevere, even in the face of strong adversity, because of their convictions. They are dedicated to overcoming obstacles, relentlessly pursuing their goals. Duckworth argues that grit is a better predictor of success than IQ or family income. People with grit refuse to quit.[36]

Moses is a great example of a biblical personality who had grit. Although he spent his early years in cultured Egyptian society, he never abandoned his simple Hebrew roots. After Moses' exodus from high society, he didn't have an easy life. He killed an Egyptian who was beating a fellow Hebrew. This situation caused Moses to run deep into the desert, where he became a shepherd. This was no easy life. To make a living, he had to wander the harsh desert, tending a flock of sheep. God didn't lead him into the dessert after he killed the Egyptian, Moses chose to isolate himself. Yet God chose to reengage Moses in a miraculous manner using him to lead the Israelites out of Egyptian slavery. A quick summary of Moses' life reveals he was a man with grit because he persevered, fulfilling his purpose. Over the course of his life, Moses encountered many complicated problems that certainly tempted him to quit:

1. **Moses'** sister, Miriam, died.

2. **He failed** to obey God's instructions when he struck the rock to miraculously produce water. This angry outburst

---

36   Fiona MaCrae, "Does true grit actually exist? Research suggests it may decide how much we achieve in life," *The Daily Mail*, April 28, 2013 (http://www.dailymail.co.uk/news/article-2316174/Does-true-grit-actually-exist-Research-suggests-decide-achieve-life.html).

cost him a place in the Promised Land; God told him that he would die before he stepped foot on it.

3. **He was denied** the right to travel on the King's Highway through the land of Edom and forced to take the long way to the Promised Land over even more difficult terrain. This must have been incredibly discouraging.

4. **Moses'** brother Aaron, died.

5. **He was constantly** on the move, which was stressful for his family and himself. He was a man without a home. He was exiled from Egypt and would never step foot in the Promised Land. For the second half of his life, Moses was a drifter, moving from place to place, leading millions of people who were also living in tents, waiting and wandering for decades.

If you add up the pain and problems Moses faced, it's obvious Moses had wounds. He could have been a defeated man, but he had grit and persevered. He could have quit, but he stuck it out and fulfilled his purpose.

Moses was able to persevere because he had grit—and he was able to find peace and rest in God's supernatural presence. Moses wrote, *"Lord, you have been our dwelling place throughout all generations,"* (Psalm 90:1).

A dwelling place is not just a house with a roomy garage and a manicured lawn. A dwelling place is a place of safety, protection, and peace. Moses didn't have a dwelling place on earth. He was a wanderer in a harsh environment. His family members died, he lost his right-hand man, and he knew he would never step into the Promised Land. All of his dreams and opportunities had passed away, one by one, with each passing day. Moses knew God was his only dwelling place. It was a lesson he had to learn the hard way.

Moses knew that before there are any pastures to graze, mountains to climb, people to lead, lands to conquer, or houses to build, there is the very presence and security of God Himself. Your security is not to be found on earth, anymore than Moses' security was found in the desert he wandered. Your security is not found in your family, home, job, or even your church. Things change, people change, circumstances change. Everything changes. Your dwelling place is in Christ because Christ does not change.

Number Your Days

This may sound weird, but I like walking through old cemeteries to look at the names and dates engraved on the headstones. Some headstones are very simple with just a name, date of birth, and date of death. Others have family member's names on them or military insignias. I wish I knew what took place during the dash, that period of time between when the person was born and when he or she died.

While traveling, Kathi and the kids and I stopped in a small town just outside of Louisville, Kentucky to walk through a really old cemetery. My kids found this detour much less enjoyable than I did. People buried in the center of the cemetery had lived in the 1800s. It was interesting to read their names and ponder how they may have lived and the problems they struggled through. One gravestone stood out to us. It had a small wrought iron fence around it with a simple gate, and it was well kept in comparison to the rest of the cemetery. The headstone was much larger than all the others. Inscribed on the stone was a woman's name with the date of her birth, death, and one sentence that said, "A noble woman and a personal friend of President Abraham Lincoln." Her whole life was summed up in one sentence that merely said she was a friend of the president. I don't know anything else about her except for that one fact written in stone for the world to see.

Cemeteries are a powerful reminder to invest the time you are given wisely because you are only given so much of it. Only God knows when your life on earth will end. When I look at the days I have spent and the days that may or not be in front of me, I am challenged to make the most of the days I am given.

What are you going to do with the rest of the time you have been given? Are you going to spend it staring at your wounds wishing things were different or do your best to fulfill the purposes and opportunities God has graciously given you? I know God has a great future in store for you. Now it's time to start living it.

Model Your Life After Jesus

Several years ago, I toured a renowned art museum in Europe. There were hundreds of pictures from dozens of respected seventeenth- and eighteenth-century artists as well as numerous modern ones. The first floor was full of abstract art, something I have yet to understand or appreciate. But the second floor was loaded with beautiful works of art. There were paintings of nature and daily life spectacularly captured in oil and other media. As I strolled along gazing at the art on the walls, something caught my eye. In the corner of a very large room on the second floor, an artist had an easel propped up in front of a picture. I walked behind the artist to figure out what she was doing. What I witnessed caught me a little off guard, the modern artist was painting her version of an ancient painting.

At first, I thought it was kind of strange to be painting a picture of a painting until I realized that the artist was attempting to capture the essence of the original artist. She was trying to blend the same colors and capture the right dimensions as the original artist. She was trying to copy the original master painter, translating it to the best of her ability onto her own canvas. And when her picture was complete, it would hopefully accurately reflect the original, priceless painting on the wall of the museum. If she did a really good job, most people would be hard pressed to tell the paintings apart.

We don't know what Jesus looked like, but the Bible still paints us a beautiful picture of Him. We know He was caring, kind, compassionate, and loving. We know He was a man of prayer and purpose, and that He was obedient to the Father. We know that He understood the Scriptures and lived them out in His relationships. The Bible paints a picture of Jesus for us to copy to the best of our ability on our life canvas. Is it possible that if we really take a close, careful look at Jesus, long enough to take in His characteristics, we will see what we can become?

Be Wonderful

The human body has a remarkable way of healing itself because that is how God designed it. If you smash your finger in a car door, it swells and turns black and blue. Your fingernail may even fall off. But over time, it will heal. It may take a month or a year, but eventually, your finger will look just like it did prior to smashing it. You will never forget the pain you felt when you hurt your finger, but the wound will not be visible.

Other wounds leave visible scars. One fall day, I was out cutting wood with a chainsaw. I have used a chainsaw for years without incident but that all changed in a fraction of a second. I was cutting a large piece of wood when the log rolled. This caused the chain to hook my left pant leg, my boot, and my flesh. It all happened so fast there was nothing I could do about it. The chain saw had made a four-inch gash in my ankle that was down to the bone. At first, it didn't hurt, then it did. It hurt really, really bad.

I managed to get into my truck and drive to the doctor's office. They quickly escorted me to a room where a doctor examined my wound and assured me she could sew it back up. But she could not sew my flesh back together until the wound was clean. She sent in a nurse, who proceeded to take a cloth and scrub the inside of the wound. The nurse told me it was going to hurt and he was right. It hurt so bad my eyes watered like crazy. The cut was so deep that he had to dig around in it with his finger to get all the wood chips out. After he finished, he called the doctor back into the room, and she stitched me back up. About a week later, I went back to the doctor so she could remove the stiches.

Today I still have a large scar on my right leg that will never go away. The good news is it no longer hurts. It is a visible sign of the trauma that took place. I still cut wood on a regular basis, but I am much more cautious.

Wounds turn into scars, and each scar tells a story. Some scars may not be visible, such as a painful period of depression or loneliness. Other scars, such as a divorce or bankruptcy, may be visible.

This book was written because I needed to clean some of my wounds so they could heal. My life is full of scars, some visible, some unseen. They are all part of my story, just as your scars are part of your story. They remind you of what happened, but they don't define who you are now.

Moving from wounded to wonderful is a choice you can make. You can experience a wonderful life. You can be the person God created you to be. You can break free from past wounds and live a joyful life. It will take time and effort, but now you have the tools you need.

ABOUT *the* AUTHOR

John Braland grew up in Minnesota and joined the United States Air Force after high school serving in the U.S. and abroad. After being honorably discharged, he attended Crown College where he met Kathi and married her a year later. John and Kathi have three awesome children: Josh, Sara, Katie; two black labs; and two noisy parakeets. John enjoys riding his Harley and snowmobile, tinkering on a zillion projects in the garage, playing hockey, and mentoring other leaders.

John serves as the President of International Ministerial Fellowship (IMF), a global organization with over 1,300 members that include military chaplains, pastors, parachurch workers, and missionaries. In his role with IMF, he is able to mentor other leaders and consult with churches helping them to make disciples and strengthen leaders.

John has a B.A. in Pastoral Ministry and an M.A. in Organizational Leadership from Crown College. He also earned a Doctorate of Ministry in Executive Leadership for Larger Organizations from Bethel University. He is ordained with the Christian and Missionary Alliance and with International Ministerial Fellowship.

John would love to connect with you!

In addition to serving as a pastor, he also does church consulting and personal leadership coaching.

Contact John at jbm@freshwaterchurch.org
or check out his sporadic blog
and videos at www.johnbraland.com.